The Essentia Blockchain

GW01457861

Blockchain

From Bitcoin to Solana to Kaspa

A comparative view of different blockchains from those emerged to emerging

Ross P. Green

The Essential Guide to Blockchain Platforms

by Ross P. Green

Dedicated to my daughter, Belle

Thank you for trying to understand blockchain

Contents

Preface

Due to the dynamic evolution of blockchain technology and its relatively youthful status, there is a noticeable dearth of literature on emerging blockchains, distinct from the well-documented cases of Bitcoin and Ethereum. Faced with the absence of comprehensive resources on platforms like Solana, Bittensor, or Kaspa, I took it upon myself to compile a singular, cohesive book to disseminate knowledge on these groundbreaking technologies.

While YouTube videos can offer valuable insights, the dispersed nature of information often necessitates sifting through numerous sources. This book consolidates data across various blockchain platforms, eliminating the need to navigate disparate videos or peruse individual volumes burdened with extraneous details that may be neither necessary nor memorable.

Acknowledging the vast landscape of over 200 existing blockchains, it is impractical to encompass all of them within the confines of this book. Therefore, I have sought a balance between well-established blockchains and those in the nascent stages of development. The terms "emerged" and "emerging" are used to distinguish between those with significant adoption and those still in the early phases, not widely recognized globally within the blockchain community.

The decision to delve into "emerged" chains is not intended to replicate existing documentation but aims to shed light on their existence and the problems they aim to address. This, in turn, provides a context for understanding the raison d'être of emerging chains.

For readers contemplating investments in the native cryptocurrencies of these chains, comprehensive information is provided throughout the book including the tokenomics. I maintain impartiality regarding investment and technological preferences for any blockchain, offering information for the reader's consideration. Therefore, there is no correlation for the blockchains described to what I'm invested in either financially or technologically.

It's essential to clarify that while I am personally invested in some of the primary focus blockchains in this book, such investments do not extend to every blockchain featured. The selection criteria involve a blend of personal interest and the broader fascination of the blockchain community.

Given the vast scope of blockchain technologies, the book does not delve into highly technical details, development levels, or algorithms extensively which may be the case for a book dedicated to a single blockchain. Instead, it strikes a balance between readability and detail, aiming to provide enough information for a foundational understanding without overwhelming the reader. The intention is to give the reader enough detail, but not to completely bend their mind!

As the blockchain space evolves rapidly, future editions or additional books may explore other blockchains. Recognizing the challenge of capturing real-time developments, the References section at the end of chapters directs readers to further details and the latest news.

To maintain accuracy, some experts and CEOs from the blockchains covered have reviewed relevant chapters. I trust you will find this book both enlightening and thought-provoking, encouraging further exploration and inquiry.

Introduction

The objective of this book is to cater to individuals with a foundational understanding of blockchain technology, offering them an opportunity to deepen their knowledge by delving into newer emerging blockchains and comparing them with established counterparts. A basic proficiency in blockchain concepts, including a high-level understanding of how blockchains operate, familiarity with terms such as forks, and comprehension of consensus mechanisms, is assumed. Additionally, readers are encouraged to possess some knowledge of Bitcoin and Ethereum, along with an acquaintance with cryptographic concepts like hashing and public and private key encryption for digital signatures.

While the book accommodates raw beginners, a smoother experience is anticipated for those with a grasp of these basics. Although certain areas are explained and in layman's terms and supported by simple analogies, prior familiarity with these concepts enhances reader engagement.

The narrative of this book unfolds the evolution from well-established blockchains to emerging ones, each attempting to enhance aspects such as security, scalability, or decentralization. Notably, certain emerging chains, like Bittensor for AI and Sei for Decentralized Finance, introduce diverse functionalities.

The surge in blockchain and cryptocurrency developments has led to a multitude of platforms seeking to elevate scalability, security, decentralization, or create foundations for varied applications such as Decentralized Finance (DeFi), AI, or NFTs. After the inception of Bitcoin, Ethereum emerged with a mission to amplify scalability while laying the groundwork for smart contracts and decentralized applications (DApps). The inherent tradeoff between scalability, security, and decentralization, commonly known as The Trilemma, became apparent, posing a challenge for many blockchains.

Addressing this challenge, various emerging blockchains employ innovative approaches. Kaspa, for instance, tackles the scalability limit by allowing parallel block creation, demonstrating comparable security and decentralization to Bitcoin. Kadena claims to have resolved The Trilemma by enabling parallel chain creation through Proof of Work mining.

A newly emerging blockchain, Saito, challenges the conventional notion of The Trilemma, proposing it as an economic limitation rather than a technological one. According to Saito, the predominant incentive problem in most blockchains, where budgets are primarily allocated to security through mining or staking, hinders scalability and decentralization. Saito's unique solution involves rewarding nodes beyond mining and staking, promoting a self-sustaining network.

Saito claims they have solved the Trilemma by basically suggesting that there is no Trilemma! The details on Saito are covered much later in this book, but in many blockchains only mining nodes and staking nodes get paid, which is great for the security of the network but what about scalability and decentralization?! Nobody is paid for this, and rather, most blockchains are challenged with enhancing these two facets of the Trilemma. As an analogy for incentives, what if a painter gets paid to pick up the paint, but not to paint the walls? If there is no incentive to paint the walls, then how will this turn out? Likewise, if there is no economic incentive to scale or decentralize because nodes are not rewarded, this yields an incentive problem.

How about if scalability and decentralization are paid for? How about nodes other than mining or staking nodes get rewarded for this contribution? This is what Saito attempts to solve, a network that pays for itself rather than people (in the form of volunteers or pure altruism) paying electricity and infrastructure costs to run their own nodes with no economic incentive.

Other blockchains such as Sei aims to optimize a specific sector such as DeFi and trading applications and as a result can finalize transactions very rapidly. Also, the Algorand blockchain can finalize transactions instantly and there is no possibility of a fork!

The ongoing evolution in solving The Trilemma and creating application blockchains, such as AI for Bittensor, presents a captivating and continually evolving landscape showcased in this book. By combining technological insights with details on the tokenomics of each chain, readers may find valuable perspectives to inform their investment decisions.

The decision to focus this book on Layer 1 blockchains was not only to provide a foundation for understanding different blockchain technologies, but to consider why they have become so valuable. If one looks at the top 100 cryptocurrencies by market capitalization, there is a pattern in that about 80% are layer 1s and the remaining are layer 2s and other application tokens and meme coins. This may tell you something. It tells you that the layer 1 coins are seen by the market to have utility and therefore, value. After all, layer 1 coins are used for transaction fees, securing the network and governance. This is immediate and obvious utility. The same cannot be said so easily for other tokens and although some have utility, this requires extra intensive research to discover the real use for the crypto token. Of course, it depends if you are a long term or short-term investor and what your goals are, but this is a pattern that is likely not a coincidence.

Throughout the book, I aim to spark thought-provoking discussions without strong biases. The various claims, criticisms, and insights presented are attributed to blockchain experts and founders, fostering an open and balanced exploration of diverse perspectives. I want to clarify that these are not my criticisms or claims, but that of others.

This book strategically poses numerous open-ended questions to provoke contemplation among readers and foster a receptive mindset. This deliberate approach aims to encourage reader engagement, acknowledging the nascent stage of the technology discussed. It is important to note that certain questions presented may currently lack definitive answers, owing to the evolving nature of the field. Over the passage of several years, these inquiries have the potential to find resolution.

Attempting to provide conclusive responses to these questions in the present moment may be deemed unrealistic, given the dynamic and transformative landscape. A pertinent illustration of this uncertainty is evident in Ethereum's recent transition to Proof of Stake and the forthcoming implementation of sharding. Given the recency of these developments, predicting the precise outcome remains elusive. In contrast, Bitcoin, particularly at its foundational level, benefits from the accrued wisdom of time, offering a more solid foundation for concrete answers to emerge.

As a final note, this book primarily focuses on Layer 1 blockchains, foundational platforms where DApps can potentially run. Interoperability chains (Layer 0), such as Cosmos and Polkadot, and other concepts like Layer 2 chains and applications or sidechains, fall beyond the scope of this book.

The Trilemma

One main aspect of this book regarding blockchain platforms is the Trilemma. There are three critical components for a blockchain platform to function and those are security, decentralization and scalability. The challenge with all blockchains is to balance these three components so that they are all enhanced as much as possible without any trade-off.

The Three Aspects of the Blockchain Trilemma

The reality is the three aspects of the Trilemma are intertwined such that maximizing one component usually results in diminishing another. This creates a predicament for software developers who must then trade-off one of these components to enhance the other two. The Trilemma is such that there can only be two pillars optimized out of the three and so the third one will not be optimal like the other two. Essentially, optimizing one aspect results in the expense of another, making it challenging to achieve all three simultaneously. Let's take a look at these aspects a little more to understand why this is.

Security

The first cornerstone of the blockchain Trilemma is security and is essentially the most important, especially given that the largest application for blockchains at present is cryptocurrency where large amounts of funds are stored. However, even if the use case is not cryptocurrency, it's still crucial to ensure the integrity and protection of data, for example in the case of supply chains or ID verification.

Decentralization

The next cornerstone is decentralization which relates to the distribution of making decisions, control and data across a network of many participants (or nodes) without needing to rely on a central authority. Each node has a local copy of the blockchain ledger where any change to the ledger, such as new transactions added, requires **consensus** across those nodes. As a result, there is no need to trust a centralized entity and no single point of failure.

Scalability

The final cornerstone is the ability for a blockchain to process an increasing number of transactions without sacrificing speed and at a low cost, even as the network grows. As more users join the ecosystem and therefore initiating more transactions, the blockchain needs to handle this without huge delays, which is important for high adoption. Scalability helps to ensure that transaction fees remain low for users, otherwise the fees can increase significantly when there is congestion. This again is crucial for adoption if one wants to make the blockchain desirable for users and developers. In addition, a scalable blockchain provides a smoother experience for users which would otherwise lead to frustration and loss of trust.

Although it's not strictly the case most blockchains tend to tackle the facets as a priority in the order just described being security, decentralization and scalability. There is no point having maximum scalability if the platform is not secure! Of course, that is not say that scalability is developed last in the roadmap as all three facets would likely be worked on and designed in parallel. However, in blockchain and most technologies in general, scalability tends to be the last (and often most challenging) issue addressed as usually in the early stages of a project the priority is to get a product working and a proof of concept demonstrated. A blockchain platform can still go into production without high scalability, as long as it scales enough to work. This has clearly been the case as the vast majority of blockchains have few security issues but currently most cannot scale very well.

The following illustrates the Trilemma in terms of the three facets for a blockchain to function:

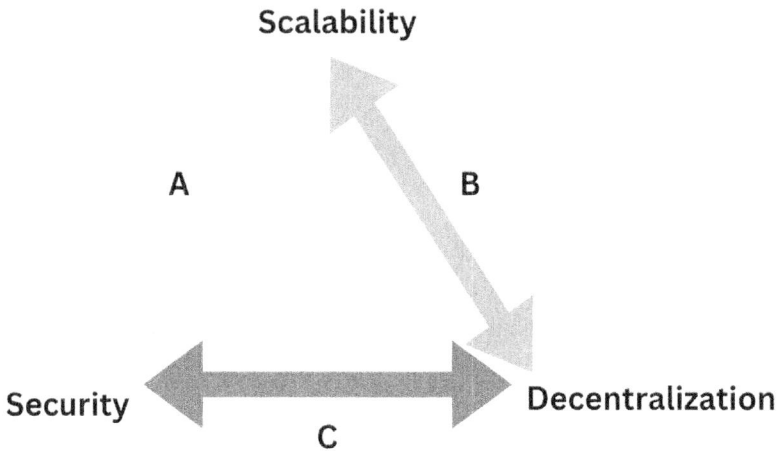

Scalability

A   B

Security   ⟵————⟶   **Decentralization**

C

With the Trilemma, there can only be two pillars optimized before diminishing another, and therefore it's a design choice which two are enhanced and which one is compromised. In the diagram above it shows that two points of the triangle can be chosen with the other being diminished. For example, if one wants high security and decentralization, as per the triangle one may need to compromise on scalability. Another example is choosing (or enhancing) decentralization and scalability results in a compromise on security, the reason for which is described in the next section where increased scalability generally requires compromising security. Essentially, the Trilemma triangle diagram shows that choosing two points of the triangle moves away from the other point (hence a compromise). The challenge of course, is to maximize all three with no compromise.

Some blockchains claim to have solved the Trilemma by ensuring that increasing one pillar doesn't diminish another. However, this is still subject to much debate and cannot be totally proved until those chains have achieved mass adoption. Some have achieved it on their test networks (called a testnet) but it remains to be seen if this is still the case in a production environment (called a mainnet). Those blockchains that have claimed to have solved the Trilemma are featured in this book and are notably Kaspa, Kadena, Saito and others.

Why does enhancing one pillar compromise another?

Now that we understand the three main pillars, let's look into why enhancing one pillar diminishes another, from a technological viewpoint. For example, increasing security usually results in diminishing scalability and this is not a blockchain specific issue, but also a technological issue across the whole space. Anyone who has worked in software development in other applications would have experienced similar issues and certainly the Internet itself showcases this on many fronts.

The security and scalability trade-off

In cryptography (Note, this technology existed way before blockchain, and is used in many applications for securing connections to web servers for example) data is encrypted and decrypted. There are two types of encryptions:

Symmetric encryption: Uses the same digital key for encrypting and decrypting data, the simple analogy being like a single padlock key for a treasure chest.

Asymmetric encryption: A different key is used for encryption and decryption being a private key and a public key. These two keys are linked mathematically. Therefore, an owner with the public key that mathematically corresponds to the private key can decrypt the message. In the context of blockchain it decrypts to reveal a hash to verify authenticity of the sender who signed the transaction.

Asymmetric encryption is more secure and in the context of blockchain, it's used for encrypting digital signatures whereby any node with the public key can verify the authenticity of the message sender, because only the message sender has the private key. The public key can decrypt messages without any knowledge of the private key, thus there is no intrusion. This is why it is suitable for blockchain technology. If the same keys were used (as would be the case with symmetric encryption), then any node with the key could encrypt and verify the signatures. This would be a problem because there would be no way to verify the authenticity of the sender as anyone could sign the message, for example in the context of a transaction. In blockchain the public key is sent as part of a transaction and that key can only verify a digital signature (signed by the initiator of the transaction) for the corresponding private key (that the initiator owns). Essentially the private key proves ownership and enables spending of funds and the public key verifies the legitimacy of the digital signature.

In the context of asymmetric encryption however, the private and public key are mathematically related using some clever and beautiful mathematics trickery of prime numbers. In essence, this means that whoever has the public key (related to the private key) cannot determine the private key, and of course this is critical because, after all, the private key is meant to be private! It should only be known the by sender (in the blockchain context, the initiator of the transaction to send Bitcoin for example). Without going into detail, it's based on the concept in mathematics that given two prime numbers, if you multiply both these numbers to get a result, it is basically impossible to determine the two prime numbers used to get the result. Now applying this for a private and public key, it's impossible to determine the private key from the public key because they are mathematically related using prime numbers. This is a simple explanation as there is more involved than just prime numbers, but this gives you an idea of how complex mathematics is used to relate the keys.

Now that asymmetric encryption has been explained, let's use an analogy for the Lehmann to understand why increasing security diminishes scalability. It's clear that complex mathematics is used for encryption and decryption and even more so for asymmetric encryption due to the mathematical binding of the public and private keys. This requires more intense mathematics, complexity and therefore computer instructions. Therefore, in very simple terms, imagine for your house you have many different locks for door and windows where each has a separate key. This is more secure because there is no master key to unlock all doors and windows! You may also require two different keys to unlock a single door. Although this is more secure, it's also slower as accessing your house each time requires an extra key to unlock the door. Much like apartment blocks have a key to unlock access to the building and another to unlock your own door. Therefore, someone with only one key cannot access your house as they need both. It's clear that the time consumed to unlock access to the house is slower as more and more keys are required, albeit more secure. This is an extremely simple analogy, but helps to translate to the context of software which is essentially not very different. The more secure and complex encryption algorithms used the slower the execution. This addresses the balance and trade-off required between security and scalability, which are two facets of the Trilemma. The use of public and private keys in the context of a transaction is described more in the Bitcoin chapter.

To be clear, the example just described is not an issue as such with blockchains because all blockchains use asymmetric (public, private key) encryption for digital signatures, but still showcases how extra security can hinder scalability. Many blockchains use other modules and measures to increase security overall for their respective ecosystem (outside of digital signatures), but this can affect scalability. It all depends on what the blockchain sets out to achieve and thus needs to align its design with its goals. This will become clearer upon delving into the blockchain chapters later in this book.

As an example of a blockchain where a push for scalability has come at some expense of security is Solana which has achieved a high number of transactions per second. However, this has not been without some pain as Solana has suffered some vulnerabilities resulting in funds lost. There are two ways to view this where one could say this is a no pain no gain approach as Solana has pushed the boundaries and this can be seen as a positive where the result is very high scalability. On the other hand, funds have been lost and it's not a good perception for the Solana blockchain. Bugs in software are normal, but blockchain bugs can have catastrophic consequences due to huge amount of TVL (total value locked) on chain.

The decentralization and scalability trade-off

As described earlier a decentralized network does not rely on a centralized entity and therefore, for this to work there needs to be many nodes involved in consensus when a new block of transactions is proposed. Since there are many nodes, this increases chatter between those nodes and it takes time for all the nodes to synchronize.

There are different consensus mechanisms such as Proof of Stake and Proof of Work where the latter requires intensive resources to finalize and agree between the nodes. There is more detail on these consensus approaches later in the book. However, as the number of nodes increases the time required to reach consensus also tends to increase, which leads to higher latency and therefore a decrease in the number of transactions processed per second.

In a decentralized network, each node must validate transactions and in the case of Proof of Work this requires significant computational power and even more when the network grows. The more nodes there are the more time it can take for transaction data to propagate across the network, which then results in delays.

Many of the blockchains featured in this book have solutions to mitigate the effect of delays, latency and chatter between nodes. For example, Proof of Stake (increasingly used by many blockchains) requires a 2/3 majority vote of a set of nodes on a rotation basis to reach consensus, unlike Proof of Work. This means not all nodes are required to vote in a given window of time and so helps to make the network more efficient. There are many other solutions to the decentralization and scalability side of the Trilemma, and these are described later in this book in the various blockchain chapters.

However, one solution that some blockchains use to increase scalability is to dramatically decrease the number of nodes required to participate in consensus. BNB smart chain (BSC) has only 21 validator nodes for reaching consensus which although makes the chain very efficient, it also makes it very centralized. This is an example of a trade-off made in this part of the Trilemma. BSC has in the past paused the whole blockchain as a result of a security issue and this can be seen from two different angles. The first angle is that with a small set of validators it makes it easy to coordinate between them and pause the chain to resolve problems. On the other hand, this means there is centralized control and this goes against the principle of blockchain in the first place. Pausing the whole blockchain doesn't seem an ideal approach each time there are issues and is tantamount to the idea that other controls could be put in place at the disadvantage of the users.

As a final note, increasing centralization also tends to lead to decreased security because nodes can collude together more easily in a malicious manner that could negatively affect the blockchain. This is known as a 51% attack and is discussed later in the book. This would be an example of another trade-off in the decentralization and security part of the Trilemma, whereby increasing centralization decreases security.

A modular approach to solving the Trilemma

Blockchains are generally built using a monolithic approach where nodes carry out many tasks such as validating transactions, ordering transactions, verifying disputes and finalizing blocks. A blockchain is a decentralized network of nodes that collaborate to validate the order and legitimacy of transactions within a block and the blocks themselves. A modular approach, such as that taken by Celestia, separates these functions.

The four core functions of blockchains

There are four main core functions of a blockchain and these are laid out below:

Execution Layer: This is where applications built on the blockchain reside and transactions are therefore executed with the state of the chain updated.

Consensus Layer: This is where ordering and validity of transactions occur.

Data Availability Layer: This layer is responsible for the record of transactions and published transaction data being available for download.

Settlement Layer: This layer finalizes transactions in blocks after being submitted by the execution layer for disputes and proofs.

Typically, a monolithic blockchain has all the four functions built into one layer. Some blockchains take the execution function to a separate layer called a Layer 2 where computations are performed off chain and uploaded as a batch (rolled up with the results) to the layer 1 main blockchain later. This helps to reduce the load on the Layer 1 chain. However, the main problem is by combining all the functions in a single layer requires a collective responsibility for nodes to reach consensus, ensure data availability and execute transactions. As a result, attempts to optimize one function consequently leads to the demise of another because a node focusing on one task or function takes the focus off another, hence a trade-off is needed. This is because execution, consensus, availability and settlement are all competing for the same resources and leads to inefficient execution, bloating of states and high gas fees. As per the Trilemma, this is a trade-off to the scalability pillar.

Blockchains such as Celestia decouple execution functionality from consensus ensuring that the consensus layer is just required to order transactions and guarantee data availability.

Decoupling Execution from Consensus

Celestia decouples the layers so that there are now separate modules for the execution layer, settlement layer and consensus with data availability layer (note the latter is in one module). With this approach each layer specializes to perform its own function in an optimal way to allow increased scalability for example.

The following illustrates the approach taken by modular blockchains like Celestia of separating execution, settlement and consensus:

Monolithic	Modular
	Execution Layer
Execution, Settlement, Consensus, Data Availability	Settlement Layer
	Consensus and Data Availability Layer

The solution that Celestia use consists of different types of nodes to carry out the separate functions. It uses light nodes where these nodes don't contain full blocks but instead, they use a technique called **data availability sampling**. This enables them to check random parts of a block to make sure that data is available without requiring the whole block to be downloaded. This allows the light nodes to detect invalid blocks such as where data has been withheld by block producers. This is an example of performing verification of a block required for the consensus function (one of the four core functions of a blockchain).

Those more familiar with Bitcoin may ask "How is this different to Bitcoin or other chains that also use light nodes?". The main point is that Bitcoin light nodes (called Simple Payment Verification nodes), although also don't contain full blocks, just check if a transaction is in a block, but don't verify the validity of the transactions or detect invalid blocks. This extra check requires the full nodes (that have a full copy of the blockchain) to perform this validation.

Over the course of this book, the modular approach isn't described much further, but highlights the fact that there are many different ways to tackle the Trilemma. The modular approach that Celestia uses is also relatively new. The general approach taken by most blockchains currently is to separate functionality using either a Layer 2 or a sidechain. This doesn't separate all four core functions outlined earlier, but Layer 2s for example decouple the execution function from consensus to increase scalability. Many of the blockchain platforms discussed in this book use a Layer 2 or sidechain to address the challenges with the Trilemma. Although Layer 2s and sidechains are mostly outside the scope of this book, they are highlighted in some of the chapters to illustrate how this approach helps with scalability (such as the Bitcoin chapter). A large part of many solutions to the Trilemma are addressed at the layer 1 itself, and since this book is about layer 1 blockchain platforms, that will be the main focus.

Is the Trilemma a Technological or Economic Problem?

The Trilemma is largely seen by the community as a technological issue. This is not unique to the blockchain space as anyone involved in software development knows very well that scalability usually comes at the expense of other areas such as security for example. Scalability is always a challenge for any technology project, but before blockchain it was able to be solved more readily as most solutions used a centralized model and therefore there was no need to consider decentralization as compromising scalability. With the advent of blockchain technology however, there were now two large factors hindering scalability, being the level of security and decentralization. In summary, less security and more centralization allowed scope for more scalability.

However, a blockchain project called Saito (featured later in the book) claims that the Trilemma is not a technological issue as such, but an economic one. This is largely because security for almost every blockchain is intact due to the economic energy used by nodes (validators and miners) to secure the chain. These nodes are rewarded for securing the blockchain and thus provides an incentive to maintain security. In most blockchains though, there is usually no reward or economic incentive to keep the respective chain decentralized or scale highly. This results, unsurprisingly, in these two pillars (decentralization and scalability) suffering somewhat.

The Saito solution is both economic and technological where the technology model supports the blockchain economy to reward efforts for all pillars of the Trilemma, not just the security pillar. The nodes contributing to decentralization and scalability also get rewarded. The details are described in the Saito chapter, but it's certainly a unique way of approaching the problem. As a result, Saito essentially claims there is no such thing as a Trilemma as such, but rather it's related to a lack of incentives for decentralization and scalability. If users were incentivized for their efforts for these pillars, the overall issue wouldn't exist.

Consensus Mechanisms

Consensus Mechanisms Overview

There are many consensus mechanisms, the main two being Proof of Stake and Proof of Work. Proof of Stake has gained popularity due to its energy efficiency. However, it may be a surprise to many that Proof of Work in Bitcoin can potentially help the environment. This is described in more detail in the Proof of Work section. There are other Consensus Mechanisms such as Proof of Routing Work used only by Saito (described in the Saito section later in this book) which is a very unique approach to consensus. Solana uses Proof of History (described in the Solana section). For this section only Proof of Work and Proof of Stake are described with some interesting discussion points as a warmup and to reinforce knowledge you may already have on this topic.

There is a lot of documentation on this topic so, to minimize the bloat of this book I will touch briefly on certain aspects so that the focus can be on the newly emerging blockchains and other insights. Therefore, the description of PoW and PoS are more a recap and suitable for beginners in the space. The pros and cons of both Proof of Stake and Proof of Work are described later in this section.

Proof of Work

Proof of Work is the consensus mechanism used by Bitcoin, Kadena, Kaspa and various other blockchains. Proof of Work is a solution to the Byzantine Generals' problem (and Proof of Stake is a different solution) of how to reach a consensus across a decentralized and distributed computing environment.

First, let's understand the Byzantine Generals' problem. The problem relates to a group of Byzantine generals, each commanding a portion of an army, who are around a city they intend to attack or retreat from. The generals need to reach a consensus on whether to attack or retreat, and they must do so in the presence of potential traitors among them. The challenge is to develop a consensus algorithm that allows the loyal generals to reach an agreement even when some of the generals may be traitors, where they may send contradictory messages to confuse the outcome.

The problem in a simple summary, is how do we coordinate people (in the case of software, nodes) across a large region, when those people (or nodes) are spread out globally without the honest people (or nodes) having to trust every other person (or node), where some may be dishonest in the either nearby but more so, remote locations?

The following depicts this problem. In a distributed computing world, think of the coordinated attack as an agreement by consensus for those nodes to achieve a certain goal as per the rules of a program and think of the traitors as misbehaving computer nodes who may not follow the programmed rules. This is a coordinated attack resulting in victory:

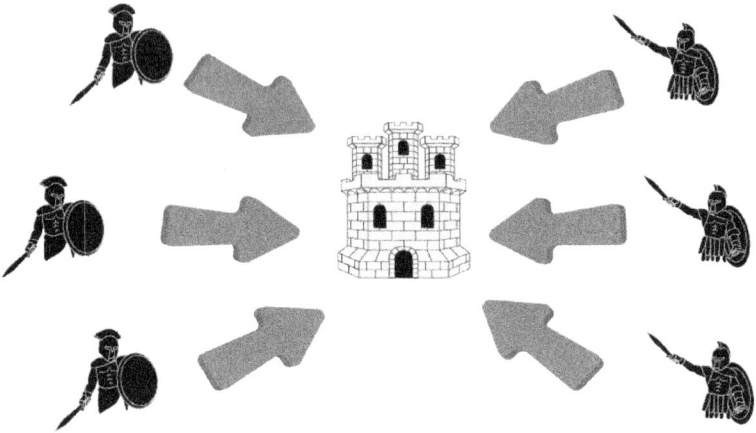

This is an uncoordinated attack resulting in defeat – the green arrows indicating those who betrayed:

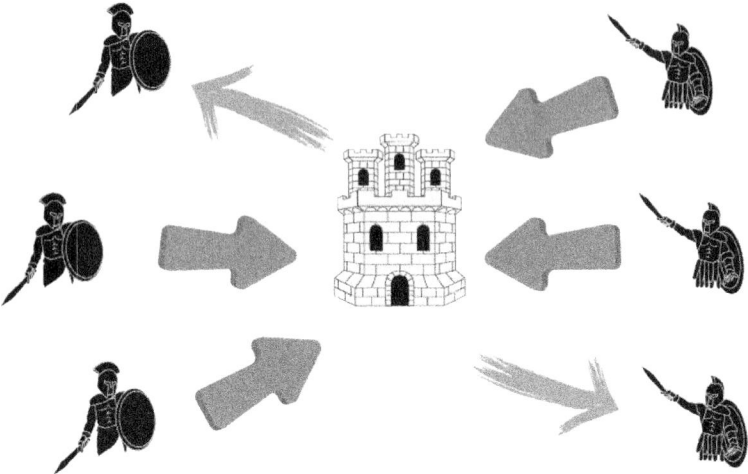

So how can we avoid the situation in a distributed computing world where traitors (misbehaving computer nodes) compromise a goal to reach consensus? One such way to reach consensus is Proof of Work which requires an expensive computer calculation, and this is the process known as mining. Mining must be performed to create trustless transactions on the blockchain.

A consensus mechanism such as PoW that solves the Byzantine Generals Problem thus achieves Byzantine Fault Tolerance (BFT). This addresses the challenge by ensuring that the distributed system can withstand a certain level of faulty or malicious nodes without compromising its correctness and reliability.

PoW in summary works as the following:

- Transactions are broadcast to the network by nodes, then the nodes in the network verify these transactions to check they conform to the rules of the blockchain.
- Transactions are bundled up together in the form of a block by a mining node. These transactions are selected from a pool of unconfirmed transactions, with those with the highest fees selected as higher priority.
- Miners (mining nodes) then verify transactions for each block, checking to see if they are valid.
- Miners solve a mathematical puzzle known as proof of work. The puzzle is a difficult mathematical problem where a hash needs to be calculated with a certain number of leading zeros. The network has a predefined difficulty level that determines how hard it is to find a solution. Miners need to find a solution that, when combined with the block's data, produces a hash that meets the difficulty criteria.
- If the puzzle is solved, the miner broadcasts the block to the network for other nodes to validate, that is the block and its contents
- Once all validated, the block is then stored on the blockchain where that block is linked to the previous block. Of course, this block contains the verified transactions.
- The miner is rewarded with a block reward and fees for those transactions to be included in the block.

The following illustration depicts this:

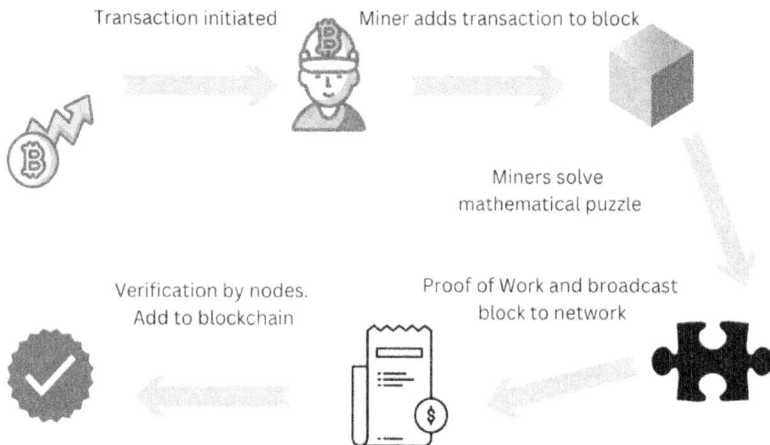

The question that most new to the blockchain tend to ask is "Why do the nodes have to solve such a complicated mathematical problem as a base for consensus, surely that's not good for the environment?". The answer is, it doesn't have to be this way, because there are other consensus mechanisms such as Proof of Stake that reach consensus without having to solve this problem. However, Proof of Work is a very strong solution to the Byzantine Generals Problem because it's very difficult to game. It's a way of proving that a significant amount of work has been done, and the node (or pool of nodes) that has produced the most amount of work is rewarded which helps to secure the blockchain as there is an incentive to keep the node(s) honest. As an analogy, think of the guy at the gym that has worked hard lifting weights and leaves the gym all ripped with huge muscles. This is very difficult to disprove, the evidence is clear he did the work! Likewise, a computer mining rig can prove this by solving a complex mathematical problem. This makes the network very difficult to hack because a node(s) would need to do even more work (using computational power, thus electricity) to create a block with malicious transactions.

To expand on this and clarify a little more, the benefits and some advantages of Proof of Work (with respect to Proof of Stake) are listed below:

Financial Incentives

Miners are economically motivated to act honestly. PoW has a huge cost because it requires significant power, therefore electricity, due to solving complex mathematical problems. Miners are therefore rewarded with cryptocurrency coins, known as the issuance, and the transaction fees in the block. This creates an incentive which aligns with the security of the network, because miners have an interest in remaining honest by following the rules if they want to receive rewards.

Decentralization

PoW allows anyone with the required computational power (hardware and electricity) to add new blocks to the blockchain. This open participation ensures that no single miner or group can control the network promoting a more decentralized distribution of computational resources.

PoW encourages a competitive nature that ensures that miners are always competing to solve complex mathematical puzzles to add new blocks. This competition prevents the dominance of any single miner or miners because other miners are always trying to participate and earn rewards.

Note that this is the idea and concept to achieve decentralization, but in practice there are large mining pools that control large portions of the computational power. However, so long as the incentive structure is good enough this negates a possible 51% attack because this attack would likely result in the miners losing more than the rewards they receive, due to the electricity costs and decline in the price of the cryptocurrency they are being rewarded in. This point is expanded on in the Mining and Staking Pools section later in this chapter.

Immutability of Transactions

Once a block is added to the blockchain, modifying it becomes very difficult. For an attacker to modify a block, they would need to modify the block concerned and recalculate the proof of work for that block and all previous blocks linked to it. This level of computational effort makes the blockchain highly resilient to modification.

Security and Prevention Against Double Spending Attacks

PoW helps to prevent double-spending attacks (spending the same amount of money twice) by providing a way for reaching consensus on the order of transactions in the blockchain. Once a block is added to the blockchain, it is linked to a chain of blocks. The cumulative proof of work makes it computationally extremely difficult to create a different chain with conflicting transactions.

Network Difficulty Adjustment

The network's difficulty level adjusts dynamically based on the total computational power (hash rate) of the network. This adjustment makes sure that, in general, a new block is added to the blockchain at a stable rate. If there is an increase of miners joining the network, the difficulty increases, and if there is a decrease, the difficulty decreases. This helps to maintain the security of the network and the stability of the network.

Hash power, often referred to as computational power or hash rate (measured in hashes per second), is the measure of how much computational work a miner or a group of miners can perform per second. It's a measure of the processing power required to solve mathematical problems being cryptographic puzzles and hashing algorithms.

The higher the hash power, the more computational work can be achieved, therefore, the higher the probability of successfully mining a new block.

How PoW in Bitcoin can help the environment

Although Proof of Stake has been popular due to its energy efficiency, I thought it worth discussing how Proof of Work in Bitcoin can help the environment. I think it's clear Bitcoin mining uses lots of energy (although there is a significant portion of clean renewable energy as miners seek to reduce costs) and there is an abundance of information out there on this, so this book won't rehash that. However, there is less information on how it can benefit the environment. For Proof of Stake, it's a no brainer (because it doesn't use huge computational resources), so that's why Bitcoin's PoW has been emphasized here. It's a little outside the scope of this book, so this section is very brief, but again I think it's an interesting insight to stimulate your thoughts.

Essentially, there is an intermittent nature to solar and wind energy, because they only produce energy when the sun shines and the wind blows. A lot of this energy is generated when demand is low, so there is an oversupply of energy. Now, if this energy is not stored in batteries, it is basically wasted. The miners can purchase the excess energy from solar and wind farms, which of course increases the revenue of those renewable companies, and it also prevents taxpayers from subsidizing all that extra energy.

In summary, Bitcoin mining rigs can be switched on where there is an oversupply of energy, thus absorbing the energy that would be otherwise wasted and thereby redirecting the electricity from the grid to the mining rigs to mine Bitcoin. The rigs can then be switched off when there is an undersupply of energy and so redirect the energy back to the grid.

As a final note, in addition to renewables, Bitcoin miners can also help stranded methane (which is a potent greenhouse gas) which is not economically efficient to bring to market. Methane comes from gas and oil operations and landfills. The key to all this is that Bitcoin miners can operate in any geographical location where they can turn the stranded methane into electricity, then use that to mine bitcoin producing an environmental and monetary benefit.

Proof of Stake

There are many variants to Proof of Stake (PoS), but those are tackled later in the book as those blockchains that use PPoS or DPoS for example are described. This will give more relevance and context rather than describing every PoS variant in advance.

PoS is a consensus mechanism which is a variant of how to solve the Byzantine Generals Problem to PoW. It's used to achieve agreement on the state of the blockchain where it determines the creator of a new block based on the amount of cryptocurrency a participant has staked as collateral.

These participants, known as validators, are required to lock up a certain amount of cryptocurrency as collateral, known as their "stake." This stake serves as a commitment to the network and is held as validators perform their duties.

Validators take turns proposing and creating new blocks in proportion to the amount of cryptocurrency they have staked. The more the validator has staked, the higher probability they have of being selected to create a new block.

There are different methods for selecting the validator to create a new block and this varies among different PoS implementations. Some use a randomization process based on the stake, while others use the length of time the cryptocurrency has been staked (coin age).

It's more energy-efficient compared to PoW because it doesn't need the same amount of computation, therefore electricity consumption. Validators are chosen based on their stake rather than their ability to solve complex mathematical puzzles.

PoS networks implement security measures to deter malicious behavior. For example, validators may be punished and lose a portion of their stake if they are caught acting dishonestly.

The PoS mechanism in summary works as per the following:

- A user places a stake of tokens into a staking pool, thus locking them up as collateral.
- The next validator is chosen based on their stake size in that the probability being chosen is proportional to the number of tokens they have staked. There may also be another element in that length of time they have been staked for has an effect (coin age). This also increases their chances of being chosen. However, the system may reset this periodically to prevent a validator dominating the network by always proposing blocks.
- The chosen validator proposes a block consisting of transactions in it.
- Other participants get to approve and verify the proposed transactions in the block. If there is misbehavior such as double spending or proposing invalid blocks the validator may be punished and have their stake (all or part) slashed as a result.
- A new block is then linked into the blockchain.
- The validator earns a transaction fee (Note that in Ethereum this will also be a block reward, known as the issuance, and also MEV rewards. More detail on this in the Ethereum chapter).

The following illustration depicts this:

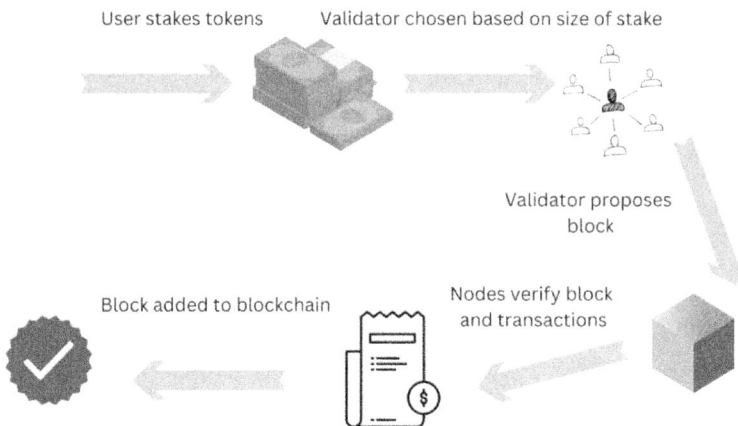

User stakes tokens   Validator chosen based on size of stake

Validator proposes block

Block added to blockchain   Nodes verify block and transactions

37

In the Ethereum chapter and other blockchain chapters that use PoS, the details of aspects such as voting, penalties, checkpoints and fork choice rules are fleshed out in more detail. However, as a high-level summary consensus can be achieved with no issues if less than one third of the validators are dishonest. What this means can be summarized in two points:

- If more than 1/3 of the validators are dishonest then the chain could be paused. If this happens the dishonest party may choose to not partake any further, meaning the rest of the validators will not be able to uphold a 2/3 majority (which is needed for consensus). This leads to no transactions occurring at all.
- If more than 2/3 of the validators are dishonest then collusion and bribing could happen. This situation is extremely undesirable because the blockchain now suffers from things such as double spending of transactions and other attacks because the 2/3 majority has control.

Of course, this leads to making sure there is a huge set of nodes in the network to lessen the chance of collusion, but this is at odds with scalability because this now requires lots of chatter (and therefore delays) to achieve consensus across the large set of nodes in the network. Some methods to avoid such scenarios are rotating validator committees (providing a subset of validators selected from the main validator set), Slashing and Penalties, and Proposer Builder Separation (PBS) among others which are discussed later in the book.

Further to all this, the benefits and some advantages of Proof of Stake (with respect to PoW) are listed below:

Security

Validators have a financial stake in the network because they need to lock up tokens as collateral to receive rewards such as fees, MEV or a block issuance. This discourages malicious behavior, as validators risk losing their funds and rewards if they act dishonestly.

Energy Efficiency

PoS is generally more efficient than PoW in terms of energy consumption. PoW requires miners to solve complex mathematical puzzles thus using lots of energy and resources, but PoS relies on validators to create new blocks where they are chosen based on the amount of cryptocurrency they hold.

Cost Reduction

PoS reduces the need for expensive hardware and electricity. This makes it more cost-effective for participating nodes. Those in PoS blockchains don't require powerful mining rigs, and therefore ASICs, GPUs or any specialized hardware, which lowers operational costs.

Scalability

PoS is considered more scalable than PoW because it doesn't have the same level of computational limitations, which leads to being able to handle a larger number of transactions. Therefore, with fewer computational hurdles, PoS can potentially offer quicker finality for transactions. However, as this book reveals, some more advanced PoW approaches using DAGs can achieve higher scalability.

Reduced Risk of Centralization

Although this is highly debatable one may say that since PoS doesn't rely on computational work, there is a lesser risk of centralization. This is because in PoW, in regions where electricity is cheap and mining hardware is more affordable, there is an increased tendency to become more centralized. Also, only those with deep pockets and expertise in mining hardware have the ability. PoS opens to the wider masses because all that is needed is the ownership of some cryptocurrency tokens, albeit often a large number. Either way, money is required, either to stake or buy mining hardware. However, with PoS one doesn't need the same level of expertise setting up large mining rigs.

Proof of Work vs Proof of Stake

The following illustrates PoW and PoS side by side for an at-a-glance comparison:

	PoW	PoS
Mechanism for Consensus	Mining	Validating
Rewards	The node that mines a block receives a reward.	The node that is chosen to validate and propose a block gets a reward.
Security	Provided by hashing to solve a mathematical problem to propose a block.	Staking collateral to propose a block.
Malicious Activity	No explicit rules for punishing bad actors.	Activity by bad actors results in the stake being slashed and penalties.
Efficiency	Less efficient. Renewable clean energy is encouraged for cost saving.	Energy efficient.
51% attack approach	Must control 51% of the hash power.	Must control 51% of the staked collateral.
Equipment	ASICs and GPUs	Standard server grade devices

In both PoS and PoW, they (miners and validators) earn transaction fees for the transactions they include in a block.

However, for Ethereum 2.0, in addition to these rewards, there is an issuance block reward like Bitcoin (although it was reduced since Ethereum 2.0 where it moved from PoW to PoS) and validators can also earn MEV (Maximal

Extractable Value), which is the amount of value that can be extracted from a block by reordering transactions. MEV is earned by validators who can extract value from the transactions they include in a block. More on this in the Ethereum chapter.

There has been much detail so far on some advantages of PoW, and this was emphasized somewhat more because it appears less obvious to many, so the objective of this was to provide some stimulating insights. However, the following describes advantages and disadvantages for PoW and PoS:

	Advantages	Disadvantages
Proof of Work	Can encourage use of renewable energy Proven over time	Expensive Equipment required High Energy Usage Slower transaction speeds
Proof of Stake	Energy Efficient Less Expensive equipment required Less expertise regarding equipment	Unproven at large scales or long periods Can require high investment to stake

Note that it's mentioned that PoS is unproven at large scales or long periods, especially given that Ethereum recently moved to PoS and can't dramatically scale thus far. After five more years this situation may change. Other blockchains may well be able to scale, but don't yet have the level of adoption like Ethereum and are still relatively new.

Regarding scalability for PoW, this situation is also changing as solutions using DAGs and parallel chains are achieving higher speeds.

41

Mining Pools vs Staking Pools

Mining pools are groups of miners who combine their computational power to mine blocks where the rewards are paid in proportion to their contribution. So even if a miner's individual computational power is low, mining pools are useful because they allow miners to receive more consistent rewards.

Staking pools are similar to mining pools, but they pool together the staked tokens of multiple users which increases the probability of earning rewards rather than using computational resources. Staking pools have a lower barrier to entry because one doesn't have to stake large amounts of tokens or run a validator node.

However, just to be clear, mining and staking pools, although similar, are not the same thing. With mining pools, they don't take custody of the ASICs, the miner itself owns and takes custody of the ASIC hardware. Therefore, a miner can simply switch their hash rate (computational power) and point somewhere else within seconds.

With staking pools, they in many cases take custody of the validators. This means that if a pool is controlled by a centralized entity (for example an exchange), you may not be able to switch and point to a different pool quickly and therefore, can be quite sticky. Many have limits and it can be days to wait before one can switch to a different pool. Payouts also can be delayed and in extreme situations if the centralized entity has financial issues, it's theoretically possible that one may not get paid rewards at all because the centralized entity has control. Of course, in the case where there is no centralized entity this isn't an issue, but currently it's quite common that an exchange is involved.

However, mining pools in Bitcoin for example, do have a level of centralization as also do staking pools in Ethereum. Centralization in this context is not ideal, although some would argue that because the incentive structure in Bitcoin is very sound and predictable, there is little or no motivation for a 51% attack, thus the miners and mining pools are kept honest, or could be known as benevolent whales. The incentive structure in Ethereum is also a sound one, although perhaps less predictable because since Ethereum 2.0 there are also MEV rewards which introduce a variable APY, and a reduced block issuance reward.

If one considers the cost of an attack especially in Proof of Work whereby there is an electricity cost, but also the decline in the price of the cryptocurrency (as the market finds out about the attack), most calculations reveal that the cost is simply too high. Markets tend to react very quickly, so it's likely that a selloff will happen so quickly, that the attacker may not be able to realize their profit before the selloff occurs. Either way, it's a huge risk. But in both cases, the security budget and therefore, the reward structure seems sound enough to deter any motivation for a 51% attack. I will leave this an open question for you to ponder.

The current distribution for Bitcoin mining pools is shown below:

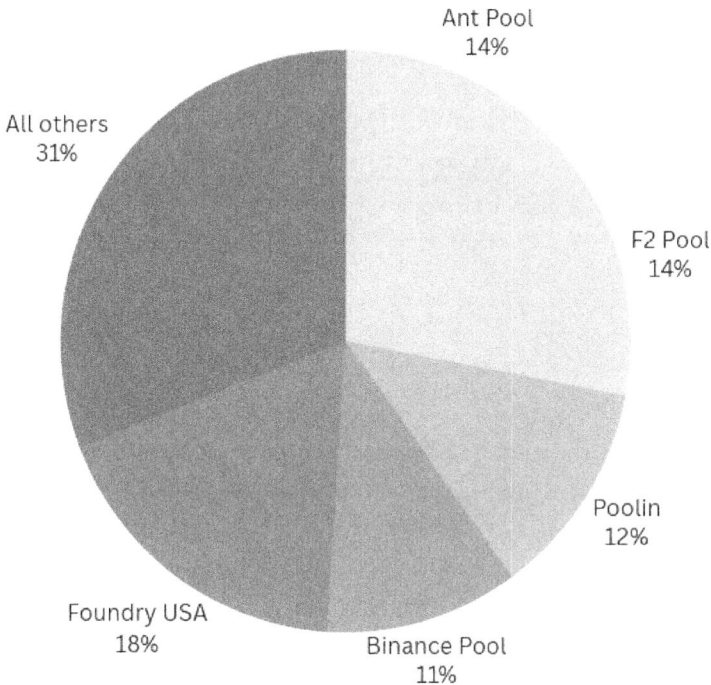

Ant Pool
14%

F2 Pool
14%

Poolin
12%

Binance Pool
11%

Foundry USA
18%

All others
31%

The distribution for Ethereum staking pools is shown below:

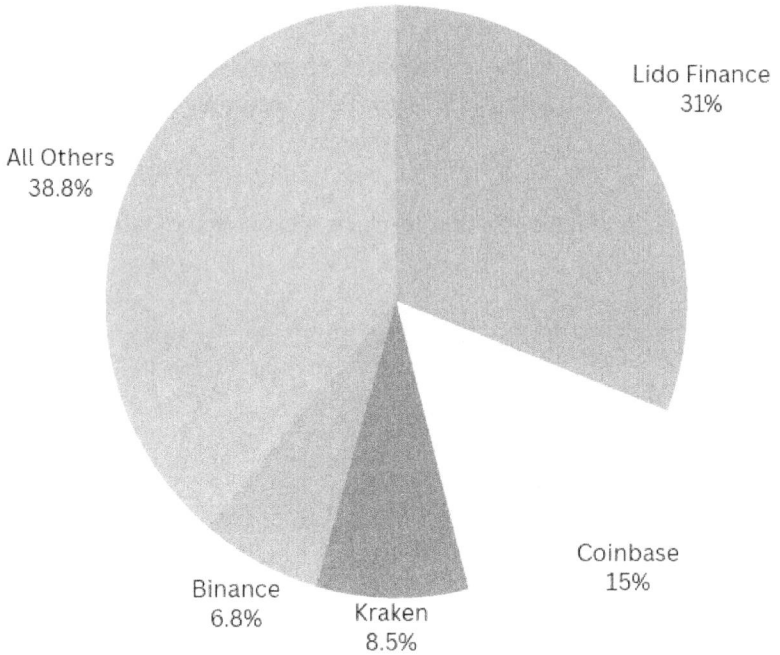

Note that this may have changed for both Bitcoin and Ethereum since the time of writing, but it shows that it's possible for large entities to have ownership control. Whether it's actually a bad thing or not depends partly on whether you think the incentive structure is good enough to deter any malicious attack such as a 51% attack. If the incentives are good enough, then we have benevolent whales, or so it appears. Let's just say, for the sake of not going down a rabbit hole, I will leave it at that!

However, a rough calculation of what a 51% attack looks like for Bitcoin is interesting, nonetheless.

Let's assume a hash rate of around 200 EH/s (exahashes per second), highly subject to change since the time of writing of course.

The attacker plans to execute a 51% attack for one hour.

The hash rate required is:

51% of 200 EH/s = 0.51 * 200 EH/s = 102 EH/s

The cost of acquiring this hash rate:

Acquiring ASIC mining hardware: Assume the cost per terahash (TH/s) is $50 per TH/s.

Cost = (102 EH/s / 1,000,000 TH/s) * $50/TH/s = $5100 per second, which is $18,360,000 for one hour!

This is a simplified calculation and does not factor in other costs like electricity and maintenance.

Calculate the potential earnings during the attack:

Bitcoin block reward is 6.25 BTC per block. With a block time of 10 minutes:

Possible earnings = (6 blocks in the hour) * 6.25 BTC + fees (but not hugely significant).

You can quite clearly see that unless the BTC price makes a significant leap, the cost of the attack far outweighs the rewards! This is exacerbated by the fact that likely the BTC price would also drop once confidence in Bitcoin subsides, so that attacker would need to liquidate quickly.

Physical Power vs Non-Physical Power

Another interesting aspect as a point for discussion is the concept of physical power and non-physical power. Physical power applies to PoW and non-physical power to PoS. The issue with non-physical power in PoS is that given there are so many rules, it yields the possibility that it can be gamed, manipulated and corrupted. In a sense, think of powerful people and governments where essentially now there is a digital government. It's hard to argue this for physical power since a physical fight cannot really be manipulated except in the rare event someone loses on purpose! If someone wins a fight, it's clear and evident. It's certainly less susceptible to manipulation.

Bitcoin created something never done before, where essentially you could now have Physical Power extending across the globe, not just being limited locally!

Some would say that PoS could be more susceptible to manipulation because where there are more rules, it creates room for manipulation.

It really depends on whether you think any rules for PoS can be gamed in some manner. One such theoretical example is that in PoW a 51% dishonest majority of miners could be overthrown by the 49% honest minority of miners because energy is basically infinite. They (the honest minority) can always get more physical power. But in PoS this is perhaps not the case. Let's say you have a 51% dishonest majority of validators that were able to collude together and a 49% honest minority. In theory, there could be a situation where this honest minority may never be able to relinquish power because it's based on the number of tokens staked. In Ethereum for example, there isn't an infinite amount of ETH. What if the honest minority were not physically able to get more ETH on the market to stake? Perhaps it won't happen in practice and even if it did the community could instigate a fork of the chain, but obviously it's not a desirable solution. This is all very theoretical but it's an open question for you to think about.

Proof of Work Chains

Bitcoin

Brief History

Bitcoin was created by an anonymous person or team of individuals under the name Satoshi Nakamoto. A domain was registered in 2008 under bitcoin.org and a whitepaper was released later that year. The motivation behind Bitcoin was largely centered around the Global Financial Crisis and centralized control that many large corporations have. There was a hint based on this when Bitcoin went live on January 3, 2009, where the first message in the genesis block said, *"The Times 03/Jan/2009 Chancellor on brink of second bailout for banks"*. This marked the first decentralized cryptocurrency, BTC, in response to a large distrust in legacy financial systems. No longer would someone need to completely depend on large powerful financial institutions, but rather one can now hold their own wealth in a wallet in a self-custodial fashion under their complete control. Nobody except the owner of that BTC can withdraw the funds from their wallet because only the owner knows the key to access it.

Bitcoin aimed to provide a secure, transparent, censorship resistant and ultimately decentralized alternative to the banking system, which is largely seen as a black box. No central authority controls Bitcoin, unlike banks and institutions, because the Bitcoin blockchain is a peer-to-peer network and therefore requires no trust of any institution or middleman.

Bitcoin has a total supply of 21 million BTC coins where this maximum supply is expected to be reached by the year 2140. BTC is created as a reward for miners who secure the network and validate transactions by solving complex mathematical puzzles. This reward halves every 4 years in the event called The Halving. This essentially lowers the inflation rate of BTC, contributing to its scarcity.

Since Bitcoin was the first blockchain, this chapter will describe some blockchain fundamentals that helps to lay the foundation for the rest of the book. It may make the read easier somewhat for beginners who have already watched a video on basic blockchain concepts. Further to that, the book, Mastering Bitcoin by Andreas Antonopoulos, lays out all the concepts in much more detail.

What Problem is Bitcoin Solving?

There are some that say, "Bitcoin fixes everything!" or "Bitcoin solves the world's problems!". This is likely an exaggeration stemming from sheer bullishness and that's ok to some extent as people get excited, but it should be taken with a pinch of salt. Bitcoin solves many problems, but it's not going to fix the world! Moreover, it was created in response to many issues regarding fiat currency and the traditional financial system and is designed to solve many shortfalls. Some of the issues are relevant to many blockchains that were built after Bitcoin, and some are unique to Bitcoin, but some of these properties and solutions are subject to debate. As the reader you will likely have your own view. Suffice to say, let's explore these one by one as per the following:

Decentralization: Bitcoin operates on a decentralized network of computers rather than a central authority such as is the case with the banking system. This means no single entity controls the network which reduces the risk of corruption, censorship, and failure. The latter is quite significant as there is no central point of failure as nodes are distributed globally in a peer-to-peer fashion. No middleman is present in a Bitcoin transaction meaning that huge value can be transferred quickly and for a very cheap fee. Some critics question the value of Bitcoin, but it surely can be said that the ability to send money around at high speed (even if this requires a separate scalability layer) for a very cheap fee is solving something that traditional finance is not. This must be a valuable proposition in response to those critics.

Sound Money: Bitcoin has a finite supply of 21 million BTC coins unlike fiat currencies that can be printed without limit. This limited supply mimics the scarcity and durability of precious metals like gold, which have historically been sound forms of money. However, it could be said it's even better than gold because one can always find more gold, but nobody can discover more BTC because it's programmed in the code! It's also more divisible and portable than gold, but more on this in the later points in this section.

However, despite initially being a solution as peer-to-peer cash, Bitcoin has more emerged to be a store of value which makes it more comparable to gold than fiat currency. This is mainly because Bitcoin doesn't scale at the base layer as it currently only achieves 7 transactions per second, which isn't suitable as peer-to-peer cash. There are other scalability solutions such as Lightning and RSK that solve this, and these are discussed later in this chapter. The current narrative is a store of value, but it remains to be seen if it will become peer-to-peer cash with other scalability solutions or perhaps even both.

Immutability: Once a transaction is confirmed on the blockchain, it cannot be altered or removed. This is the property of immutability and ensures the integrity of transactions with a history going all the way back to the first transaction, making Bitcoin great for traceability and auditability.

Censorship Resistance: Transactions in BTC can be made by anyone globally without the need for permission from banks or governments. This is because a BTC wallet doesn't require any KYC (Know your customer) or ID checks which renders it difficult for authorities to censor transactions or freeze accounts. Of course, if the wallet is on an exchange, then we are essentially back to the banking system because these wallets are not self-custodial as they are owned by the owners of the exchange which means they are custodial (not self-custodial) wallets. These custodial wallets would require KYC and ID checks as part of exchange verification. However, Bitcoin was designed at its core to be peer-to-peer and self-custodial meaning that a wallet is owned only by the wallet owner as only they have the key for the wallet to approve transactions and withdrawals.

Divisibility: Bitcoin is highly divisible, where each BTC coin is divisible into 100 million smaller units called Satoshis. This divisibility makes Bitcoin accessible for small payments for a very cheap fee, which is not always possible with traditional currencies. Again, as mentioned, due to scalability constraints small payments with BTC are not very practical but solutions such as Lightning, Tectum and other layers are working to address this.

Portability: BTC can be transferred rapidly and easily across borders, making it a global currency that isn't bound to a nation or any regulations. This can be compared to gold which is less so the case. It is true that large amounts of gold are not usually transported but rather there is a transfer of ownership in the form of a receipt. However, smaller amounts of gold, which are very valuable, are still at risk when transported and above a certain amount normally needs to be declared at airports. This is not the case with Bitcoin because all one must do is carry a digital wallet (be it a hot wallet or hardware wallet) which is extremely portable. On a final note, in simple terms, since the key for a wallet is a set of words, these can be memorized and stored in your head, meaning that your BTC is extremely portable!

Transparency: The blockchain is a public ledger, meaning all transactions are visible and verifiable by anyone. This transparency helps prevent fraud and things like money laundering. Critics argue that Bitcoin is used for money laundering, but this is a gross misunderstanding of how the technology works. Perhaps a tiny fraction is laundered, but any attempt is thwarted with huge challenges because Bitcoin (as with any blockchain) is a public ledger for all to see! The Bitcoin ledger does not induce these issues but rather solves them.

One such benefit that blockchain technology created (where Bitcoin was the first) was that of **triple entry accounting**. All subsequent blockchains of course benefit from this trait. To understand this, let's first understand briefly what this is and how it arose, and what problem it solves.

Back in history, records of transactions were kept using single entry accounting where each financial transaction was tracked as a single entry to view the flow of money. This, however, didn't provide a comprehensive view of the assets or liabilities for a business. Consequently, **double entry accounting** improved upon this by recording each transaction in two separate accounts, being a debit in one account and an equal credit in the other. This provided a balance sheet and resulted in a more systematic approach to bookkeeping to help detect errors and fraud. With the advent of blockchain technology, triple entry accounting adds a third entry which is secured cryptographically and serves as an immutable and verifiable record. This third entry specifically is the unique digital signature that is signed for a transaction by all parties involved. A blockchain records every transaction in a block where the current block is linked to the previous block, creating a chain of blocks that is visible to all users. This makes transactions easier to trace because all records are linked in a chain going all the way back to the first (or genesis) block ever created. This can provide real-time verification of transactions and reduces financial manipulation.

The bonus with blockchain technology is that the transaction from one party to another is all transparent to the public, but in addition to that, the whole transaction from the sender to the receiver is viewable in a single place within a block. This is not the case with double entry accounting because there are two accounts, where to track the flow of money and see the full scope of a transaction, an accountant must check the debit account and the credit account to tie them both together as they are in separate places. So blockchain simplifies the approach because there is no need to cross-reference separate accounts to piece together transactions.

The following illustrates double entry accounting vs triple entry accounting:

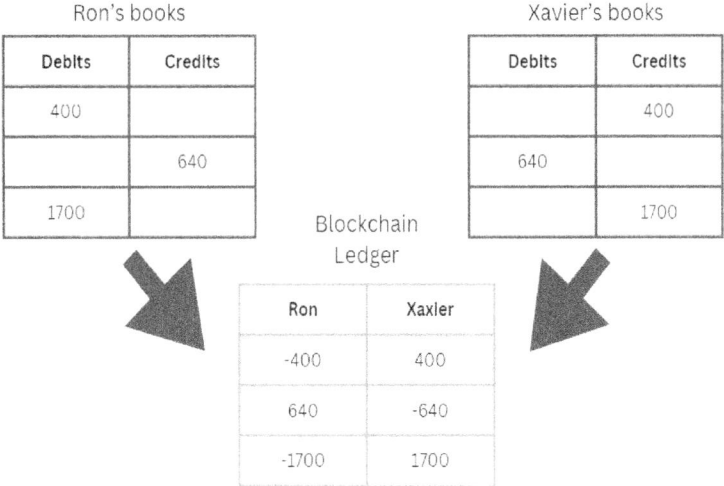

Ron's books

Debits	Credits
400	
	640
1700	

Xavier's books

Debits	Credits
	400
640	
	1700

Blockchain Ledger

Ron	Xavier
-400	400
640	-640
-1700	1700

It's clear to see that both books are essentially merged in the blockchain format. In the double entry approach each bookkeeper has their own view to maintain, but in the blockchain ledger triple entry approach all the credits and debits can be seen in one transaction (where each transaction is a row in the ledger above). This allows smoother tracking and traceability of transactions.

Security: The Bitcoin network is secured by huge amounts of computational power, making it extremely resistant to attacks and fraud. Another level of security is based on cryptography, which is a technology that existed way before blockchain. In essence, cryptography allows transactions to be verified using a form of encryption where a pair of keys are used, being a **private key and a public key**. The sender of a transaction signs and approves a message with his private key to create a **digital signature**. Any other blockchain node can verify the digital signature (to check that the sender is legit) by using the public key that is mathematically related to the private key (hence the key pair).

Thus far, since inception the Bitcoin blockchain has never been compromised. The mechanics of this is described in the "Bitcoin's Proof of Work Consensus Mechanism" section.

Many of these properties just mentioned are arguable. For example, Bitcoin as sound money is subject to large debate in the community and beyond. Many believe other blockchains and cryptocurrencies are better as money. Likewise, decentralization is widely debated, not just for Bitcoin but for many other blockchains, because decentralization is a spectrum. How many nodes need to participate or vote in consensus to be decentralized? How much ownership of a token is required by many users or entities to be decentralized? There is no definite answer as such, and it is quite subjective. However, there are calculations such as the Nakamoto Coefficient that measure the level of decentralization for a blockchain from a technology perspective. In summary, this measure calculates the minimum number of entities that would need to collude before the blockchain security is compromised. Bitcoin has the highest measure of this out of all blockchains. However, some say this measure has some potential issue and there are other ways to measure it, but nothing completely definitive. The Nakamoto Coefficient is about the best we currently have.

Overall, it's clear that Bitcoin aims to offer a form of money that is decentralized, finite in supply, immutable, censorship resistant, divisible, portable, transparent, and secure. These properties address many shortcomings of the traditional finance system. Perhaps Bitcoin is not perfect because, for example, it currently doesn't scale very well at the base layer and the BTC price is very volatile. This makes it a challenge for things like micro-payments at scale and borrowing and lending. However, there are many solutions being built on other layers on top of Bitcoin to address these issues. These are described later in this chapter.

Bitcoin's Proof of Work Consensus Mechanism

As mentioned in the chapter on Proof of Work, this is a solution to the Byzantine Generals Problem. However, PoW solutions arose before Bitcoin and the advent of blockchain technology. One such solution was HashCash developed by Adam Back which was a PoW system to prevent spam and DoS attacks. With HashCash, in the effort to prevent spamming by sending a huge number of emails, the sender of an email needs to perform some computational work. This is very easy for an honest sender but not of course, for a spammer. Satoshi Nakamoto adapted this concept to then help Bitcoin secure the network and produce new blocks in the blockchain and verify transactions.

PoW also solves the Byzantine Generals Problem which is a scenario where many participants must come to consensus where there may be some rogue parties not cooperating properly. In a decentralized world this is very difficult to solve but PoW makes sure that even in the context of malicious behavior the true state of the chain is agreed upon by the honest nodes. This provides an effective way to reach consensus without requiring a third party because mining nodes need to expend energy and resources to mine and broadcast blocks which means it's not cost efficient to attempt fraudulent transactions. It should be noted that if a node attempts any such behavior, it's not explicitly punished, but rather it has punished itself by wasting lots of time and energy. Other nodes will simply reject the block as per consensus rules and it may even be red flagged by some nodes resulting in blocks from the malicious node possibly being ignored in the future. The steps in the consensus mechanism will help to understand this more in this section.

In summary, PoW is a fundamental approach to allow nodes to agree on the state of a blockchain in a decentralized manner to prevent fraudulent activity such as double spending transactions and therefore, maintaining the security and integrity of the blockchain without requiring a central authority.

As a precursor to describing how PoW consensus works, let's first understand the difference between mining nodes, full nodes and light nodes (SPV nodes).

Mining Nodes collect transactions from a mempool (a temporary store of transactions submitted by other nodes) and create new blocks. They select these transactions based on the fees as they want collect as many fees as possible for rewards. Once it has produced a block by mining, it then broadcasts it to the network to then be linked on to the blockchain.

Full Nodes also collect transactions from the mempool and maintain a version of the mempool. They verify incoming transactions and propagate them to other nodes. They do not create blocks however, and therefore don't partake in mining blocks or expending lots of energy or computational resources. They make sure that only valid transactions are broadcast and so play a key role in the network's security.

Full Nodes maintain a full copy of the blockchain unlike **SPV (Simple Payment Verification) Nodes** which don't maintain a full copy but rather contain just the headers for each block, which is still very important for verification without requiring a full download of the whole blockchain (to conserve memory). This can be more useful for lighter clients or mobile devices and they can still verify that transactions in a block are included as the block header enables this verification.

The question becomes what is mining exactly and how are blocks produced and how is consensus reached? The following steps illustrate this and how PoW consensus works:

- **Collecting transactions**: Nodes (full or mining) process and verify transactions and submit these to a mempool, which is a temporary store. Nodes then collect transactions from this mempool.

- **Producing a new block:** Mining nodes start to form a block and so select transactions from the mempool and this is prioritized by many factors such as transactions fees for example.

- **Calculate Merkle Root:** A Merkle Tree of transactions is created which is a data structure that provides a summary of all transactions in a block. This is done by essentially hashing pairs of transactions. The **hash** at the top of the tree is called the **Merkle Root** and this is included in the header for the block. Hashing is described in more detail later in this section on Merkle Trees and Merkle Roots.

- **Prepare block header and start mining process:** The header for a block contains the version, previous block's hash, the Merkle Root, a difficulty target, a timestamp and a nonce. The **nonce** is a large 32-bit number that miners change during the mining process to generate a hash that solves the mathematical puzzle required to mine (or produce) a block.

    Miners then try to generate a valid hash value that meets the difficulty target for the network which consists of continuously hashing the block header while changing the nonce until a hash is found that is less than or equal to the target difficulty.

- **Target difficulty:** This is a number that adjusts every 2016 blocks (every 2 weeks) to make sure that the time between blocks is about 10 minutes. A lower target means higher difficulty. The more miners in the network the higher the difficulty and vice versa. This is known as the **Difficulty Adjustment** in that as more miners contribute computational power then it's likely that a valid hash (solution to the mathematical problem) will be found quicker than the 10 minutes target. Therefore, this increase in **hash rate** renders a higher difficulty for the next adjustment.

- **Find valid hash:** Upon finding a valid hash, the miner has now successfully mined a block and thus has proved that it has performed the work required by the network, hence the name Proof of Work. Upon the next block mined after this current one, this hash is inserted into the field in the block header called "Previous Block Hash" so serves to be the hash that the next block mined will reference (to link the blocks in the chain).

- **Broadcast block to nodes:** The miner broadcasts this new block to the network and nodes receiving this block verify the transactions in the block, the block's hash and other information in the block such as the block size and that the block is syntactically valid as per the consensus rules.

- **Confirmation of the block:** If the block is deemed valid, then all other nodes link it into their copy of the blockchain. The miner is rewarded with a block reward in BTC and transaction fees from transactions within that block. The process repeats in the next 10-minute window for the next block where the hash of the confirmed block serves as the previous block hash for the next block header in future. This is what links each block together in the chain. Think of it like a pointer to the previous block where that previous block also points to its previous block going all the way back in history to the first ever block created.

The following illustrates PoW in action where miners continually try to generate a hash value that meets the difficulty target:

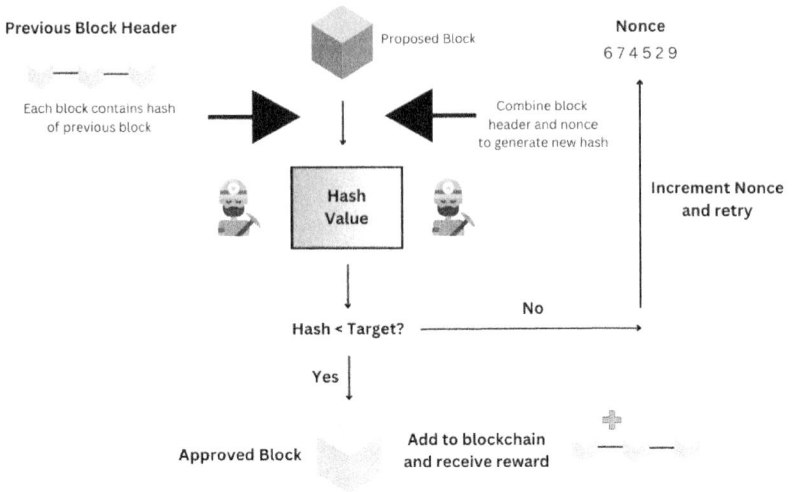

One may now ask how is Consensus reached? For example, in PoS it's basically a vote where a 2/3 majority deem the block as valid. In Bitcoin (and therefore PoW) it's based on the **longest chain rule**. The Longest chain rule in simple terms states that the valid chain is the one with the most accumulated PoW (which will be the longest chain, with the greatest number of blocks). After all, mining blocks requires work so more blocks mined means more work done, so the longest chain with the most proof of work is accepted as the valid chain by all nodes.

The system is designed such that as long as at least 50% of the hash rate of the network is controlled by honest miners then the network will converge on a single truthful version of the chain. However, if an entity controls 51% of the hash power it could be malicious and cause disruption and fraudulently double spend transactions. The decentralized nature of the network mitigates this and due to the huge computational power required to mine blocks it would be too expensive to garner the required amount of equipment and power to do this in practice. This is essentially why Bitcoin is deemed the most secure network in the world.

In summary, the PoW mechanism make sure that the network retains security by making it difficult to alter the blockchain because it's very time consuming and expensive to do so. This is because it requires a majority of the networks computing power to agree on the state of the blockchain which makes it more resistant to malicious behavior. The main point is that it's easy for other nodes to verify the work done but very resource intensive to produce that work.

Now that PoW has been outlined let's put all this together and show a Bitcoin transaction where some BTC is sent from one wallet to another. A block is proposed with the transaction added and PoW is performed to then add the block to the blockchain:

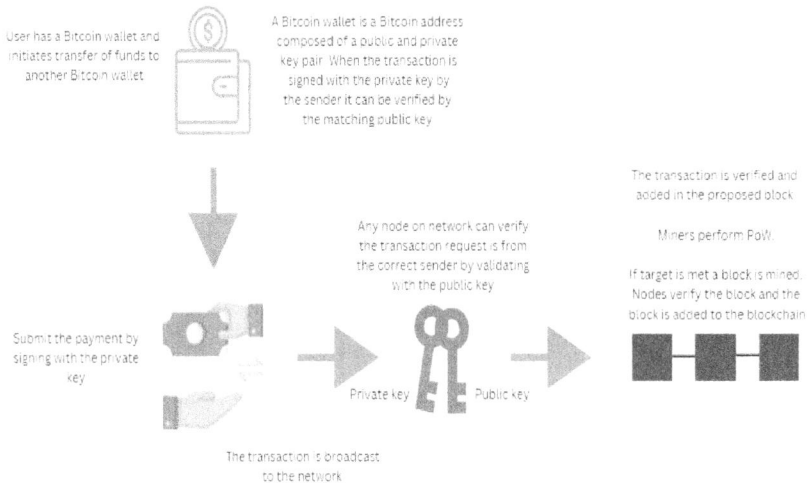

User has a Bitcoin wallet and initiates transfer of funds to another Bitcoin wallet

A Bitcoin wallet is a Bitcoin address composed of a public and private key pair. When the transaction is signed with the private key by the sender it can be verified by the matching public key

The transaction is verified and added in the proposed block

Miners perform PoW.

If target is met a block is mined. Nodes verify the block and the block is added to the blockchain

Any node on network can verify the transaction request is from the correct sender by validating with the public key

Submit the payment by signing with the private key

Private key   Public key

The transaction is broadcast to the network

The PoW step towards the end is all detailed in the PoW diagram shown earlier. This puts all the pieces of the puzzle together. So, this is the overall summary in context of a transaction:

- Once the transaction is initiated and signed with the private key, it's broadcast to the network for other nodes to verify.
- A node uses the sender's public key to verify that the sender of the transaction is legitimate. It also does other verification to verify the transaction, such as verifying the transaction's hash, available balance and that the transaction hasn't been spent twice. The transaction is added to the mempool.
- Meanwhile miners are building a block to be proposed and are extracting transactions from the mempool and inserting them in the proposed block.
- The miners perform PoW by hashing the header of the proposed block. The header consists of the Merkle Root for all transactions in the block.
- If the miner's work satisfies the difficulty target (a hash with a certain number of leading zeros), it can broadcast this proposed block to the network.
- Once the block is verified, its linked on to the blockchain. The miner receives a block reward and the transaction fees in BTC.

The mechanics of the transaction verification is described in more detail in the next section on Merkle Trees and Merkle Roots.

Merkle Trees and Merkle Roots

Merkle Trees and Merkle Roots are a fundamental part of blockchain technology and deserve more explanation as they have been mentioned so far and will be in other chapters in this book.

A Merkle Tree is a binary data structure that is used to verify the integrity of data effectively. Each part of the tree has a leaf node where each node represents a block of data, but rather than containing the data directly it contains the hash of the child nodes. The tree is built gradually by hashing pairs of child nodes until a single root hash is obtained, known as the Merkle Root.

Hashing and hash functions are essentially a mathematics concept that take data and apply it in a way such that once hashed the original contents cannot be obtained, making it a one-way function. The hash output is a condensed representation of that data and if the contents of the data were ever to be changed, the hash would change which invalidates the contents and anything (such as child nodes) connected to it. This is why hashing the data is good for verifying the integrity of data as a small change to the data results in a completely different hash output.

Due to the nature of hashing data this allows the verify the authenticity of the data without needing to check each part of the data itself. Once this is done, you now have a Merkle Proof whereby the integrity of the data can be verified for large datasets without the need for individual inspection, which is much more efficient.

The following diagram illustrates this for a set of transactions and shows the transactions, the hash of those transactions and the hash of those hashes (in pairs) until the Merkle Root is obtained. This is included in the block header and used for verification by other nodes that all transactions in the block are included and intact:

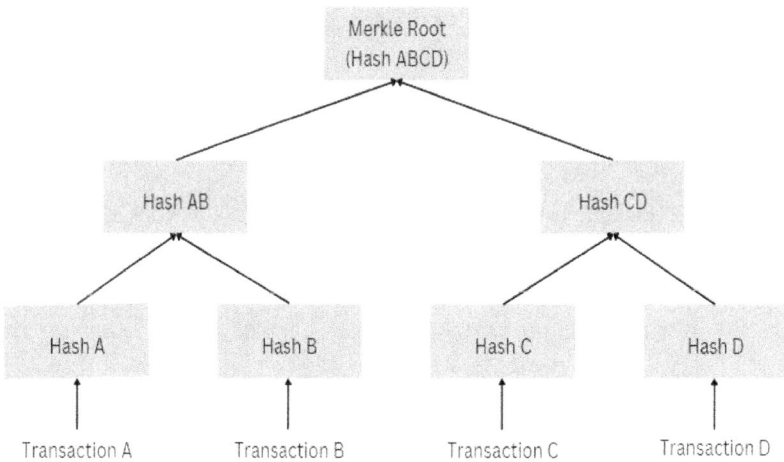

The Merkle Root represents the top of the whole tree and this is used to store block headers without requiring an entire block of information. This is also used for SPV nodes to verify data using the block header as it's more memory efficient.

The block header contains the Merkle Root (and other information such as the nonce and timestamp) and this is then all hashed (by continuously hashing the header via PoW) to form the block hash. This is then used as part of the blockchain where it points to the hash of the previous block, thus linking all the blocks together, hence the name blockchain. If a block hash changes (perhaps because data has been altered maliciously), it affects the hash of all other blocks which invalidates the chain. This is why hashing is such an efficient way to verify data integrity and to check that nothing has been tampered with.

When two blocks are mined at the same time

There can be a case where two blocks are mined simultaneously. If this happens a temporary fork (or split) in the chain occurs. Let's say there are two blocks, block A and block B mined at the same time.

This is what happens:

1. Block A is broadcast to the network and so is block B. Nodes accept and validate the first block they receive.
2. At this point the blockchain has diverged into two paths, one path with block A and another with block B, this is the point where the fork occurs.
3. Soon after nodes that received block A first, they may receive block B. However, it won't switch to block B unless it becomes part of the **longest chain**. This is a rule as part of Bitcoin's consensus mechanism.
4. Mining nodes whose view has block A at its tip of the chain will begin mining a block that extends block A. Likewise, those nodes who have block B at its tip will begin mining a block to extend block B. They are voting with their hash power. Now a race begins.

5. Let's say a node mines a new block, C, on top of B. This is propagated to the network and so nodes with blockchain containing block B at its tip receive a newly mined block, block C. This is deemed the longest chain, so blockchain B wins.

6. This is where a **reorg** (reorganization) occurs in that the nodes that had the block A blockchain now reorganize the blocks by discarding block A and linking block B, then block C to its chain. So, the nodes that were on the shorter chain, chain A, will switch to the longer chain, chain B.

7. Block A becomes an orphaned block.

8. Miners will now continue to mine blocks using block C as their parent (or previous block).

9. The transactions in block A may return to the mempool if not already in another block.

The following illustrates this situation whereby chain B becomes the winning chain with block C mined on top of block B:

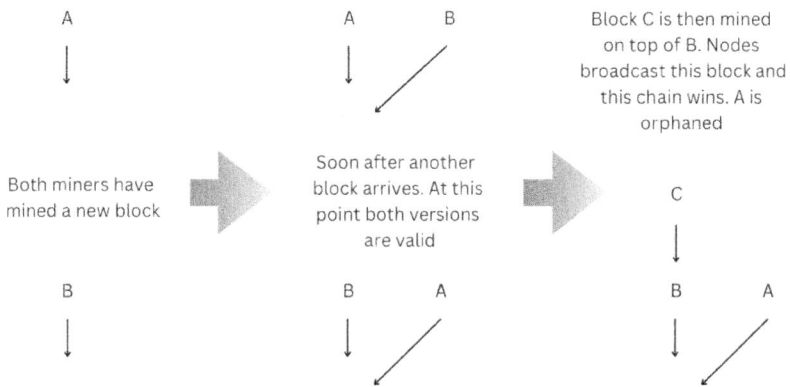

A

↓

Both miners have
mined a new block

B

↓

A   B

↓   ╱
    ╱

Soon after another
block arrives. At this
point both versions
are valid

B   A

↓   ╱
    ╱

Block C is then mined
on top of B. Nodes
broadcast this block and
this chain wins. A is
orphaned

C

↓

B   A

↓   ╱
    ╱

Bitcoin Network Architecture

The following illustrates the Bitcoin architecture that consists of mining nodes, full nodes and light (SPV) nodes:

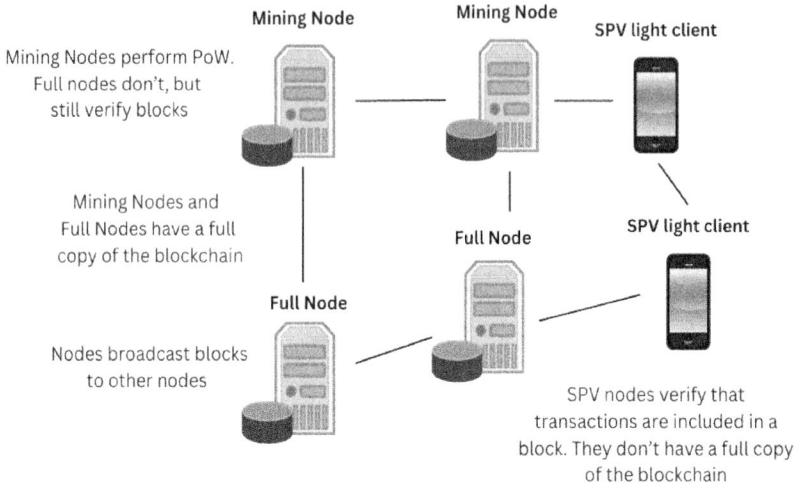

There is no single blockchain but rather every node has its own copy of the blockchain. The blue disk in the image shows a copy of the blockchain. Think of a blockchain essentially as a database with a store of all the blocks containing transactions with all the required information.

The exception is light client SPV nodes that contain the block headers only. They can still do verification of transactions through Merkle Proofs which link individual transactions to the block's Merkle Root (as the Merkle Root is contained in the block header).

What prevents someone creating a different version of Bitcoin?

A common question that gets asked is what stops someone simply creating a new blockchain with a new token for example, called BTC2, with the view of making a ton of money?! The answer is there is nothing to stop somebody creating a new chain but it's unlikely to succeed. This is because if somebody creates a new version of Bitcoin today it's likely it will be heavily attacked and compromised and so result in double spending of transactions and fraudulent activity. Bitcoin had some luck because when it first launched nobody took it seriously so nobody attempted to hack it. Then as more miners joined the Bitcoin network this meant more miners did work to solve the mathematical puzzle to create a block of transactions. This secures the network and miners received a block reward in BTC for little power consumption at the time. This steadily increased the security of the network because the amount of computational power required to solve the mathematical puzzle (a hash value with a certain number of leading zeroes) increased as more miners joined the network, thus increasing the hash rate. The **hash rate** is the amount of computational power (measured in hashes per second) that miners contribute to secure the network.

As a result, there became a point where the difficulty and hash rate were so high that it was no longer cheap to mine BTC and certainly no longer cheap to attack it due to the amount of computational power required. Any attack nowadays is simply too expensive and ludicrous to attempt.

A new version of Bitcoin could be easily attacked because it will be so cheap to carry out as there will only be a few miners at the start so a 51% attack (essentially 51% control of the hash rate) will be much more feasible. This is partly why there has been no direct alternative to Bitcoin launched with any success. The only real direct competitors that are similar are the forked versions being Bitcoin Cash and Bitcoin Satoshi's Vision and these have a much lower hash rate. They still have a decent level of security however, but not to the extent that Bitcoin has.

Other factors are that Bitcoin has essentially become a brand name and it also has a strong network effect. Once a network effect is strong, it's very difficult to displace unless a solution arises that is significantly better. The word "significantly" should be emphasized here because some solutions that are marginally better may not result in a switch of user base. Usually, if a protocol is good enough, never been compromised and has stood the test of time few users will switch to another network or protocol that hasn't stood the test of time. A similar case existed for the Internet where once TCP/IP and SMTP protocols (for email) got the network effect, even though there were perhaps some better solutions, the user base was already content with TCP/IP and SMTP.

In summary, Bitcoin has the advantage of time that has passed in that it has effectively monetized time by gradually increasing security as it garners adoption and network effects as more nodes join. The halving event every 4 years also make BTC scarcer which is great for the price. There is no way to go back in time and create a new version of Bitcoin to replicate this.

Segwit and the Block Wars

Segregated Witness was a protocol upgrade on the Bitcoin network implemented in 2017. It was a controversial point in Bitcoin's history and resulted in much community division and consequently a fork into two others blockchains, Bitcoin Cash (BCH) and Bitcoin Satoshi's Vision (BSV).

What is Segwit?

Segwit arose from much debate and contention in the Bitcoin community on how best to scale Bitcoin. Bitcoin no longer conformed to the original whitepaper because it couldn't scale and therefore it was not a viable solution as peer-to-peer cash.

It was proposed that one way to increase scalability was to simply increase the size of the Bitcoin blocks to fit more transactions within a block. The size of a Bitcoin block was 1 MB, and this was deemed insufficient by large parts of the community for peer-to-peer cash to work on a global level. The proposal was to increase the block size to 2 MB. However, this was met with resistance as a section of the community, informally known as the **Small Blockers**, were concerned this would introduce security and centralization issues and this ongoing conflict was known as the **Block Wars**. This was partly because the increase in memory usage to 2 MB increases the hardware specifications as more disk space is needed and this comes at a financial cost which could lead to only larger players with deep pockets to afford this cost thus creating more control and therefore centralization of the network. The **Big Blockers**, however, argued that the increase wasn't significant enough to price out small miners and node operators from the network and it would also make transactions faster and cheaper. This was a small compromise in their view and would also align to the original Satoshi whitepaper as peer-to-peer cash. This contention was not resolved and led to a split in the community.

The Small Blockers realized that scalability was certainly an issue and as a result they proposed Segwit which was a solution to increase the number of transactions in a block without directly increasing the block size. The solution involved removing the signature information (known as the witness) from the transaction data. This is because the digital signature was consuming about 65% of the memory space for all transactions in a block. Therefore, the idea was that by segregating the witness data from the transactions in a block allows an increase in the block size to 4 MB, thus allowing more transactions within a block. This was implemented by introducing the concept of a **block weight**, which is a mixture of the block size with and without the signature data and a limit of 4 million weight units. If this is too difficult to conceptualize, just think of it as a 1 MB limit for base transaction data that can expand virtually to 4MB to include all the witness information. The extra 3 MB contains only witness data hence the segregation of transaction and witness data.

The following shows the before and after for segwit, where in the case of segwit the separation of transactions and witness data are illustrated:

69

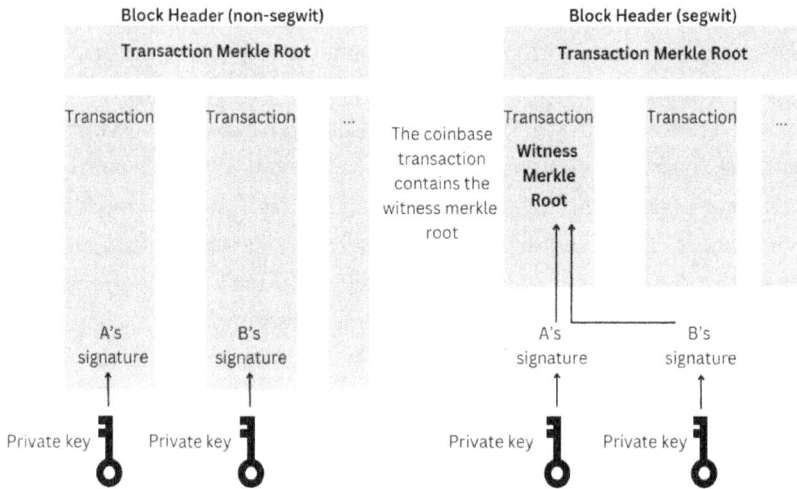

Block Header (non-segwit) — Transaction Merkle Root — Transaction — Transaction — ... — A's signature — B's signature — Private key — Private key

The coinbase transaction contains the witness merkle root

Block Header (segwit) — Transaction Merkle Root — Transaction — Witness Merkle Root — Transaction — ... — A's signature — B's signature — Private key — Private key

Note that in the interest of backward compatibility nodes can process segwit or non-segwit transactions. In the diagram above for the segwit structure, it shows the **witness commitment** which is the Witness Merkle Root and this resides in the coinbase transaction (first transaction) of a block. So, in segwit there are two Merkle Roots, one for transactions and one for the witness data whereas in non-segwit there is only one Merkle Root because the witness data is included in the transactions. One may ask, why is the Witness Merkle Root not included in the header for the block just like the Transaction Merkle Root? This is because including the Witness Merkle Root in the block header would have required a complete restructure of Bitcoin blocks and this would have broken any compatibility with older nodes that don't recognize segwit blocks (because they didn't upgrade to segwit at that point). This allowed the network to continue functioning without forcing all nodes to upgrade their software immediately.

The end result of the Block Wars

The whole debate after the Block Wars led to two main hard forks and thus the creation of two new blockchains being Bitcoin Cash (BCH) and Bitcoin Satoshi's Vision (BSV). BCH implemented a block size of 8 MB which was later increased to 32 MB and BSV forked from BCH and increased the limit to what is currently 4 GB.

The Block Wars was largely a technical debate, but it also raised a philosophical one about the grand vision of Bitcoin in terms of conforming to the original vision set by Satoshi in the Bitcoin whitepaper but also that of Governance. The Bitcoin whitepaper never specified a limit on the block size, and this was the argument especially from the BSV community. They wanted to adhere to the vision Satoshi had in mind, hence the name Bitcoin Satoshi's Vision. They claim therefore that BSV is the real Bitcoin as set out by Satoshi. It's also interesting to note that Satoshi changed the Bitcoin code at one point to set the block limit to 1 MB without any warning or explanation, and to this day it remains a mystery why he decided this. Some theorized it was to prevent a DOS (Denial of Service) attack whereby an attacker could flood the network with a very high number of transactions in the blocks (if there is no upper bound to block size) causing severe disruption to the network. This, however, has been countered by others who say that an unlimited block size wouldn't be an issue because miners need to spend time extracting transactions from the mempool to put them in a block and finding a PoW solution. If they spend all their time filling blocks with transactions (which would be the case for a DOS attack), they will never find a PoW solution to the mathematical puzzle (a hash number) and therefore will never be able to mine and broadcast that block! This would be very nonsensical and hugely costly for malicious miners. Therefore, miners would be self-regulating in theory because they would strike a balance between block size (filling a reasonable sized block with enough transactions) and finding a PoW hash solution to mine a block, which likely would level out the block size to 1 or 2 MB anyway. The idea therefore, is that a dynamic and essentially unlimited block size would cater better for changing network conditions where in times of high traffic and congestion, the block size could increase somewhat to allow more transactions and scale to meet network demand. Extremely high network demand wouldn't result in a really huge block because at some point miners need to spend time mining to find a PoW solution. This is all theoretical but was an argument for the case of having an unlimited (or very high) block size and why perhaps the DOS attack theory was not an issue after all. The truth is nobody will ever really know what Satoshi was thinking when he set the limit to 1 MB.

Overall, as a result of the increased block size and dynamic block size approach, BSV can certainly scale much more than Bitcoin but at the same time suffers from aspects of centralization and a lower hash rate due to the lower rate of adoption of BSV miners with respect to Bitcoin. The next section describes BCH and BSV in more detail.

On a different note, governance was also a point of contention in the Block Wars because the community argued that if a set of people can now decide on changes to Bitcoin, in this case the block limit, then is this going back to a centralized system like fiat currency where a group of people get to decide the monetary policies or economic model? This is discussed more in the section on "Bitcoin and Governance".

What are the differences between Bitcoin, Bitcoin Cash and Bitcoin Satoshi's Vision?

Bitcoin has been described in detail so in this section, let's highlight the vision and technical differences in terms of Bitcoin Cash and Bitcoin Satoshi's Vision blockchains.

Bitcoin Satoshi's Vision (BSV)

BSV was founded by the controversial figure Craig Wright and aims to fulfill the vision of Satoshi Nakamoto as per the whitepaper. Its emphasis is mainly on scalability through dynamic and unlimited block sizes and as a stable protocol for attracting businesses and enterprises for the development of DApps.

BSV has also incorporated smart contracts at the base layer and a **turing complete** system using the Bitcoin Script Language. In simple terms, if the system is not turing complete there can be no loops or possibility of infinite loops in the code. This is important because loops can lead to a DOS attack or a loop in the code looping forever essentially halting the system, which of course is not desirable for financial transactions! Bitcoin and its Bitcoin Script language takes this approach. BSV, however, is a turing complete system because it made updates in the Bitcoin Script language to incorporate richer functionality such as smart contracts for DeFi. It could be said that this introduces risk because loops could occur that could be exploited. However, BSV claim that they have made updates such that this is not the case because it doesn't allow infinite loops in the same way that traditional turing complete languages would do. This is subject to some debate as the introduction of turing completeness carries some risk even if it's very low. Bitcoin's approach is more conservative as it's not turing complete, albeit more limiting in functionality.

BSV has made some clever updates to align with Satoshi's Vision and although technically it could well be the more aligned and "better Bitcoin" with respect to what Satoshi originally wanted, the market has clearly not agreed. It all depends on what the vision is. If the vision is to be sound money and a store of value, Bitcoin may well have taken the better approach with its caution in updates and features. If the vision is to be peer-to-peer cash, then BCH or BSV could be better contenders due to their speed. On the other hand, the lower hash rate and therefore the possibility of a 51% attack is higher than that of Bitcoin. Suffice to say, from a technology perspective there are some impressive features that BSV has introduced.

Bitcoin Cash (BCH)

BCH was created with the goal to be a faster and less expensive version of Bitcoin and therefore act as peer-to-peer cash, hence the name Bitcoin Cash. It addresses the scalability issues of Bitcoin by increasing the block size limit (but less than BSV) to allow faster transaction confirmations.

BCH also supports smart contracts like BSV, but it lacks the turing completeness that BSV claims to be. This means that the smart contracts are somewhat more limited in their functionality and so don't support the full range of complex computations like that of Ethereum's Solidity language. This was a design choice by the BCH community to ensure tighter security.

In a sense BCH is a mixture of the security of Bitcoin and the scalability of BSV. This is because it has increased the block size beyond that of Bitcoin but not to the extent of BSV to maintain security. However, it also supports limited smart contracts but maintains a system that is not turing complete in the name of security and therefore, more functionality than Bitcoin but less than BSV.

Overall, BSV and BCH have decided to address scalability issues on the base foundation layer, but Bitcoin is addressing these issues by using separate layers such as the Lightning Network. The question is which design choice is better?

The separate layers on Bitcoin allow for decoupling of this functionality and use a concept of separation of concerns where the concern of decentralization and security is at the base layer and scalability is built on other layers such as Lightning, RSK and Stacks. Bitcoin has also partly addressed scalability at the base layer by using Segwit and so has struck a balance in the attempt to not sacrifice the security and decentralization aspects of the Trilemma. In simple terms, Bitcoin has prioritized security and decentralization over scalability because as we all know, in general, as per the Trilemma, it's hard to maximize security, decentralization and scalability all together. Usually maximizing security and decentralization will decrease (or tradeoff) scalability. So, is it better to build all functionality and scalability on a single monolithic base layer or on separate layers? Let's leave this as a thought to ponder at this point as this is discussed in more detail later in this chapter.

Bitcoin and Governance

Bitcoin's governance system is somewhat less formal than that of other blockchains where there is a Decentralized Autonomous Organization (DAO) where participants vote on new proposals.

Changes to Bitcoin are through Bitcoin Improvement Proposals (BIPs) where widespread agreement from the community and miners is required. However, the actual approach is not formalized as such. In other chains though, it uses a more structured governance model in the form of a DAO where participants with a staked token have influence on the decisions made. This can be seen as a little more centralized as per the amount of that token staked (Bitcoin doesn't formally require BTC to be held to make governance decisions) but at the same time makes the process more official and auditable. Bitcoin uses off-chain governance as part of its decision making where decisions are made outside of the blockchain system.

In the case of Ethereum it uses off-chain governance for changes to the protocol itself and on-chain governance for apps that use the Ethereum blockchain (for example Uniswap). The changes to the Ethereum foundation layer are via Ethereum Improvement Proposals (EIPs). Many different blockchain systems aim to maintain decentralization but use different methods and cultures to achieve the outcome. Some blockchains use on-chain governance for the foundation layer (hence protocol) itself.

A larger question arises from all this though. In the case of Bitcoin especially, its vision has always largely been touted to be a form of money and store of value where initially it was designed as peer-to-peer cash, but more recently as a form of hard money and store of value. Whichever is the case, one could say given that it's meant to be a decentralized vehicle of money, should there be a group of people (be it small or quite large) that get to decide on the future decisions of Bitcoin? Is this going back to the fiat model where a group of individuals get to decide on the monetary policy or financial model?

The BSV community certainly had an issue with this around the time of the block wars and segwit. They claim Satoshi never mentioned a block limit and it's certainly not mentioned in the Bitcoin whitepaper. Therefore, does a small group of individuals now get to decide a new block size for Bitcoin? BSV claim the answer is no, the block size should remain unlimited. They claim there should not be any changes unless necessary in keeping with the idea of a decentralized form of money. Perhaps the BSV community has a point here. However, it could also be seen that the Bitcoin community has struck a good balance as they have made very few changes to the Bitcoin protocol and in a very meticulous manner. If no changes were ever made this could threaten the security of Bitcoin, especially with the advent of Quantum Computing being a possible threat in the distant future, there will surely be some changes required. The BSV community could still claim that this change would be a necessary change, but the 1 MB limit on block size was an unnecessary one. It all depends on what is seen to be necessary or not. Whatever your view as a reader it's quite clear that Bitcoin makes very slow and meticulous progress with any changes, and this appears to be a good, well-balanced approach. After all, Bitcoin has never been hacked since inception and its price performance is evidence of success.

The criticism that the wider community has for Bitcoin is it's a slow technology and has very little in terms of features. But is Bitcoin meant to be a funky feature rich technology or does it mean to be a stable form of money? If Bitcoin continuously added many new features and upgrades this likely will be a threat to the stability of Bitcoin as a platform and stable form of money. Some of the confusion is that anything viewed as a technology usually wants to continuously add new features. Developers love adding new cool and funky features as do the wider community. However, some would say Bitcoin is a little unique in that although it's based on an innovative technology, being the blockchain, its vision is to be a stable form of money, not a feature rich platform like Ethereum. This leads us into the next section on discussing Bitcoin as money or as a technology with many upgrades and new features.

Bitcoin viewed as money rather than a technology

The common view with any technology is that it needs to scale and in many cases be secure, but also it must be feature rich and "move with the times". This is certainly understandable and is most often the case. Ethereum and most other blockchains for example, have a feature rich approach with many upgrades and the wider community applauds this. However, it all depends on the vision that the chain is setting out to achieve. This also comes back to the Trilemma of decentralization, security and scalability. Bitcoin sought to prioritize two facets of the Trilemma in decentralization and security, thus sacrificing scalability. The reason for this is mainly because the vision for Bitcoin is to be a stable form of money and store of value. Therefore, to achieve this vision requires a stable platform which would otherwise be compromised if Bitcoin went through many upgrades and funky new features.

Anyone with a background in IT software development is fully aware that any new change to code introduces the possibility of bugs and vulnerabilities. As a user of Bitcoin and as a store of value would you want the platform to have many new features added continuously, threatening the stability of the platform itself? Most likely you would not, especially given the traction it now has, and the amount of value stored in it. Certainly, the large hedge funds and wealth managers wouldn't subscribe to the idea of a form of money that has a threat to its stability.

Money itself should be boring if it needs to be a stable form of money. If we think of gold for example, it doesn't change form. Gold is gold and it's a very stable form of money. Bitcoin is now seen to be a digital and decentralized version of gold and therefore, it needs to be a stable platform to be a stable form of money. Note that the term stable money is more from a Bitcoin platform perspective, not a price perspective at this point because BTC itself can be very volatile. Eventually it's likely that BTC will become less and less volatile and so holistically achieving stability overall.

The next question then becomes "Can Bitcoin also be a DeFi platform like Ethereum and offer those features as well as a store of value?". In a sense the answer to this is "Yes, but not at the Bitcoin base layer itself". There is huge debate in the overall blockchain community on this topic where one camp believes in making changes at the Bitcoin layer itself to scale and incorporate NFTs and DeFi, and another camp believes it should be done on separate layers in the form of sidechains or layer 2 solutions. Examples of sidechains are RSK and for layer 2 solutions there is the Lightning network. There are also other solutions such as Stacks which don't fit the definition of layer 2 or sidechain directly but nonetheless offer feature richness to Bitcoin.

The general approach thus far is to separate the feature rich functionality and scalability on separate layers, and some would say this makes sense because making changes to the Bitcoin base layer not only threatens the stability of Bitcoin as a stable form of money but also maintains a separation of concerns. Again, those with a background in IT software architecture will understand that functionality is usually separated so that different modules and layers are decoupled. The approach of decoupling layers is largely to ensure that changes in one layer or module require little to no change in another layer. This helps to maintain the code in each layer in such a way that it minimizes complexity and doesn't require huge amounts of regression testing. For example, if all the DeFi functionality was all incorporated in one layer (in this case the Bitcoin base layer) this means the developers and testers would need to do rigorous amounts of testing to make sure that no vulnerabilities or bugs have been introduced. In the case of one large monolithic Bitcoin base layer this could get very messy and would result in "Spaghetti code" being very hard to maintain and make changes in the future. For example, all the functionality for the Lightning layer 2 was built at that layer with no changes to the Bitcoin base layer, and the same with RSK and Stacks. Therefore, it could be seen that using Bitcoin as a secure base settlement layer for transactions and using other layers to achieve feature richness is a good balance overall and leaves the security and stability of the base layer intact. Although this analogy isn't quite the same, in simplistic terms the

Internet was built on different layers for similar reasons. The core layer was IP (Internet Protocol) with layers for TCP and UDP built on top and then application layers such as HTTP (for web browsers) built on top of those.

The following illustrates Bitcoin and its different layers in the ecosystem:

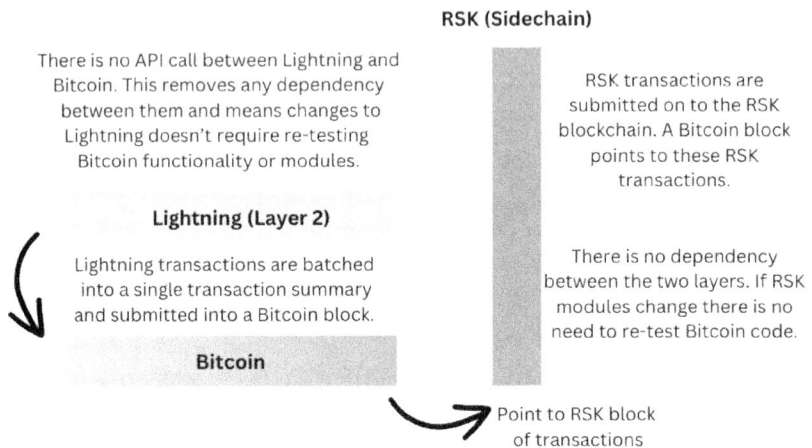

RSK (Sidechain)

There is no API call between Lightning and Bitcoin. This removes any dependency between them and means changes to Lightning doesn't require re-testing Bitcoin functionality or modules.

RSK transactions are submitted on to the RSK blockchain. A Bitcoin block points to these RSK transactions.

Lightning (Layer 2)

Lightning transactions are batched into a single transaction summary and submitted into a Bitcoin block.

There is no dependency between the two layers. If RSK modules change there is no need to re-test Bitcoin code.

Bitcoin

Point to RSK block of transactions

In the diagram above, if all the functionality was in one layer this would likely lead to modules being tightly coupled meaning that any change to DeFi features could likely result in lots of testing in foundation modules and vice-versa. In the decoupled model, however, separate layers are less tightly knit and therefore a change in a DeFi function in RSK doesn't require any re-testing in the Bitcoin base layer for example.

To expand on this a little more let's describe these other layers (RSK, Lightning and Stacks) briefly to understand how they work. You will then see that this huge amount of functionality being built all on the base layer would result in a very complex monolithic layer indeed. Other blockchains could be described as monolithic, but they don't necessarily have the objective as Bitcoin to be money as such (or a digital form of gold) so many upgrades to those platforms may be seen from a different angle as different blockchains make different design choices based on their goals. Most other blockchains don't have the vision as a form of stable money, or if they do, it's a risky approach continuously adding new features. Layer 2s and sidechains are outside the scope of this book, so for more deeper detail on these layers refer to the References in this chapter.

RSK

This is a smart contract platform that is **merged-mined** with Bitcoin where it uses the same computational power in the form of PoW as Bitcoin to secure the network. It is EVM compatible and therefore allows smart contract and DApps to be built using the same functionality as Ethereum. In the merge-mined approach miners can receive rewards in BTC and rBTC (BTC on RSK pegged 1:1 with BTC on the Bitcoin blockchain) simultaneously via block rewards and fees.

In high-level terms think of the RSK merged-mined approach as a spreadsheet in Excel where essentially a blockchain is just a database of transactions and each row in that Excel spreadsheet is a block of transactions. There is a Bitcoin spreadsheet of blocks and an RSK spreadsheet of blocks. Bitcoin blocks are mined every 10 minutes and RSK blocks every 30 seconds. Every Bitcoin block mined contains a reference to an RSK block, (which in turn points to the other recent RSK blocks mined, all in a linked chain) that is a row in the Bitcoin spreadsheet has a reference to a row in the RSK spreadsheet. This reference is the RSK tag, and it is stored in the Coinbase transaction, which is the first transaction in a Bitcoin block.

The interesting innovation in RSK is that this allows DeFi and smart contract execution to occur all using EVM compatibility meaning that it's compatible with Ethereum smart contracts. Since RSK blocks are mined every 30 seconds, essentially there are mathematical puzzles solved via PoW every 30 seconds. This is quite significant because in Bitcoin a mathematical puzzle solution is a hash value, but many hashes generated are wasted because only one block is produced every 10 minutes, so most miners PoW attempts fail to generate the hash result required. In RSK, however, a solution to a puzzle is found every 30 seconds which means more hash results are generated in a 10-minute window, leading to less waste and higher throughput as more blocks of transactions are created more often. This higher throughput is required especially in DeFi applications.

The following illustrates Bitcoin and RSK working together where blocks in Bitcoin and RSK are linked together by their separate blockchains:

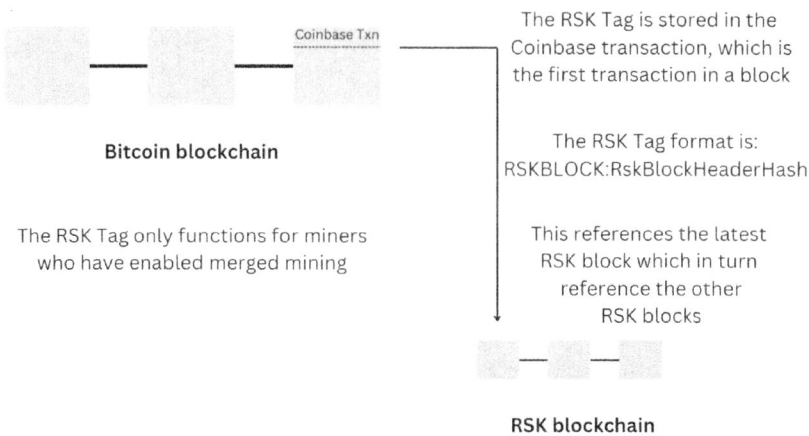

Stacks

Stacks is a separate blockchain (in a sense like RSK is a separate chain) that extends the functionality of Bitcoin to enable smart contracts and DApps to run on the Stacks blockchain itself. This has a similar goal to RSK except rather than merge-mining, Bitcoin is the settlement layer for all transactions on Stacks. Transactions on Stacks are bundled and then sent to the Bitcoin blockchain to be verified which ensures the same level of security as Bitcoin using a mining mechanism called **Proof of Transfer**. In this mechanism, Stacks miners select a Bitcoin block and include a special transaction called a commitment transaction (a transfer of some BTC) which anchors the Stacks block mined to a certain Bitcoin block. Upon this commitment, miners are eligible to mine Stacks blocks and they validate transactions for those blocks, receiving rewards in the form of newly minted STX tokens and fees. While Stacks handles its own transactions, the ultimate settlement layer is Bitcoin via the anchoring to the Bitcoin blockchain to achieve finality.

The miners on the Stacks blockchain transfer BTC to Stacks holders and this is then distributed to those holders as rewards for participating in consensus. The Stacks holders need to lock up their Stacks (STX tokens) to support the security and consensus mechanism in a process called **Stacking** and this enables them to receive the BTC rewards. The miners in Stacks are not using computational power as is thought with traditional mining but rather there is an act of committing some BTC which is then transferred (Proof of Transfer) to STX users who are stacking.

Lightning Network

The Lightning Network is a Layer 2 protocol that operates on top of the Bitcoin blockchain. The Lightning network is not a blockchain as such but enables faster transactions where a network of payment channels is used. This means that not every single transaction is recorded on the Bitcoin blockchain but rather a summary of those transactions is settled on the Bitcoin layer which also enhances privacy as the individual transactions are not visible in the summary.

The impact on security for these layers

The question that many then raise from the separate layer solutions is around the security aspect. Bitcoin has heavily prioritized security as part of its base layer design. The issue with separate layers is they are off chain with respect to the Bitcoin blockchain itself which is seen to have the highest level of security from a PoW and hash rate perspective. Although RSK essentially shares the security with the Bitcoin base layer it doesn't have the same level of hash rate as Bitcoin and is a relatively new platform compared to Bitcoin that has not yet stood the test of time. Stacks is a little different because the transactions are settled on the Bitcoin blockchain and so the lower hash rate on RSK is not the same issue with Stacks and hence this could be seen as a real strength for Stacks. However, RSK and Stacks introduce extra complexity due to smart contracts and bugs found in this area can lead to security breaches or loss of funds. A lower hash rate in RSK also makes it more susceptible to 51% attacks, where an attacker who controls more than 50% of the hash rate could double spend funds or rewrite the history of the RSK blockchain. However, in terms of the Trilemma this could be seen as a good balance and trade-off where the security of Bitcoin remains intact, and the other layers have a little less security but allows the Bitcoin ecosystem overall to be feature rich and scale.

Tokenomics

The total supply of Bitcoin is capped at 21 million BTC coins and therefore it's scarcer than gold because there is no way to find or "discover" new BTC coins. The supply is known and is part of the code and therefore this can be verified as the code is open source for everyone to check.

The miners are rewarded with BTC for verifying transactions and adding them to the blockchain. This also helps to compensate them for electricity and infrastructure costs. The BTC block reward is halved every four years in an event called "The Halving".

Eventually, of course, the reward will halve to the point where in BTC terms, the miners reward will be very low. However, if the price of BTC at this point is very high in dollar terms, it may not be an issue when considering that they also receive the fees for transactions in the block mined too.

In summary, there were no allocations of funding rounds or ICOs for Bitcoin. The only way BTC can come into existence is through mining. This makes BTC inflationary because every 10 minutes new BTC is created as reward to miners when a block is mined. However, due to the halving every 4 years, it's disinflationary meaning that the rate of inflation is steadily decreasing over time.

BTC token utility

The utility has several real-world applications because BTC provides a neutral form of money that is censorship resistant and operates independently with no central body or entity, making it difficult to seize or freeze the assets.

It can be transferred across borders with no KYC or need to ask any bank for permission. It's extremely divisible into Satoshis, which is ideal for micropayments with small fees (currently more practical when using a Layer 2 solution). An increasing number of merchants worldwide are beginning to accept BTC for payment and this may increase more once the price of BTC becomes less volatile. There are also many DeFi solutions allowing BTC to be lent and borrowed (such as Sovryn on RSK or Zest Finance or DApps on Stacks for example). It's clear that Ethereum has the larger amount of adoption in this area for ETH, but BTC is slowly garnering adoption too in the DeFi space. It remains to be seen if DeFi for Bitcoin becomes the DeFacto standard or if Ethereum or other chains have already taken the network effect for this.

Given its scarcity, BTC is ideal as a store of value like gold. The current volatility of the BTC price has caused debate as a store of value and therefore, some say it's a speculative store of value with the vision of being a non-speculative store of value (like gold) in the future.

References

The following links provide more detail on Bitcoin and its ecosystem:

Official site includes getting started with Bitcoin, how it works and running a full node:

https://bitcoin.org/en/

The Bitcoin whitepaper:

https://bitcoin.org/bitcoin.pdf

Information on RSK and how it works as a Bitcoin sidechain:

https://rootstock.io/

Information on the Lightning Network:

https://lightning.network/docs/

Information on the Stacks Blockchain:

https://www.stacks.co/

Segwit and the Blocksize Wars:

https://blog.bitmex.com/the-blocksize-war-chapter-5-scaling-ii-segwit/

Kadena

Brief History

Founded in 2016 by Stuart Popejoy (the CEO) and Will Martino, they had a vision to address scalability and security issues in existing blockchain platforms. As part of their grand vision, Kadena introduced Chainweb that uses parallel chains to increase scalability and PoW from a consensus perspective, thereby preserving some of the fundamentals from Bitcoin. Kadena also supports smart contracts, making it suitable for many decentralized applications.

Kadena launched its ICO on November 5th, 2019, and launched its mainnet in the same year.

What Problem is Kadena Solving?

In addition to solving the trilemma, Kadena's impressive focus has been its approach to increasing scalability. Kadena is a multi-chain interconnected network called Chainweb and this consists of braids of many "Bitcoin-like" chains. At launch Kadena had 10 chains interconnected but the scalable infrastructure allows it to add even more chains as adoption increases and congestion occurs on some of the existing chains. In 2020, Kadena grew from 10 to 20 chains and the team plans on expanding to a further 100 chains in the future.

The Chainweb architecture increases throughput and security where the latter makes Kadena more attack resistant. This is because an attacker would need to fork all chains in the network! This is explained further in this chapter with the understanding of Chainweb.

One can think of Kadena as "Bitcoin on steroids" as it uses PoW and a limited supply, but with many parallel "Bitcoin-like" chains in a braided fashion, thus allowing it to scale hundreds to thousands of times more.

Another unique feature of Kadena is the concept of gas stations. A gas station is an account that subsidizes all gas used in smart contract related activities for users. This makes the decentralized applications (dApps) easier to use, as users are not compelled to obtain KDA tokens from an exchange and then transfer to a web3 wallet.

Horizontal vs Layer 2 Vertical Scaling

Kadena uses a horizontal scaling approach using Chainweb rather than vertical scaling. Vertical scaling examples are Layer 2 solutions such as Lightning Network for Bitcoin or Optimism and Arbitrum for Ethereum. They are built "on top" of the Layer 1 foundation being Bitcoin or Ethereum.

The alternative approach is to scale horizontally where more parallel chains are constructed. Think of this as adding extra lanes to a highway helping to relieve traffic congestion.

The following diagram depicts vertical (Layer 2) and horizontal scaling at Layer 1:

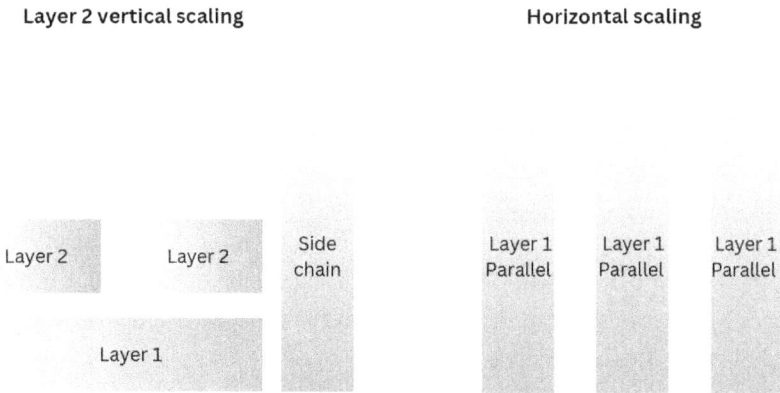

Layer 2 vertical scaling   **Horizontal scaling**

| Layer 2 | Layer 2 | Side chain | | Layer 1 Parallel | Layer 1 Parallel | Layer 1 Parallel |

| Layer 1 |

One may ask what are the reasons for deploying one scaling solution instead of another? If the base layer architecture cannot handle the existing load, a layer 2 solution essentially allows an extra layer to be built by processing the transactions off chain and rolling them up for settlement on the base layer (layer 1) later. This is what Arbitrum, Optimism and Lightning Network do for their respective Layer 1 blockchains. This passes the extra complexity to the Layer 2 solution to handle and takes the burden off the layer 1 chain.

An issue with this vertical scaling Layer 2 approach is that the security of the base chain is not reflected in the Layer 2 chain. They have separate security mechanisms. However, the privacy can be better because typically the transactions are processed in a batch and later settled to the layer 1 chain as a single transaction with a summary of the batched transactions. This is the case with the Lightning Network. There is also a different type of Layer 2 solution called Sidechains and these preserve the security by using a technique called Merge Mining, such as that implemented by RSK for Bitcoin. The Bitcoin main chain and RSK sidechain use and "share" the same consensus mechanism being PoW.

The Horizontal scaling approach keeps the security mechanism intact and all at the base layer with no extra Layer 2 solutions or sidechains. The token used can be the native token across all parallel chains. Kadena does exactly this, described later in this chapter. However, sidechains tend to use a separate "pegged" token which is not the native token. For example, RSK implements an rBTC token which is pegged 1:1 with BTC on the Bitcoin main chain. Although RSK has quite an elegant solution, this involves extra complexity such that it needs to prevent an attack whereby a user could end up with the rBTC tokens without being able to redeem the native BTC coin.

The issue with Horizontal scaling is it can also be complex in a different manner to Layer 2. Sharding for example in Ethereum is taking considerable time to roll out. There also needs to be a way to make sure all the different parallel chains are connected and synchronized. Kadena's Chainweb has a solution to this using a Petersen Graph described in this chapter.

Kadena Network Architecture

Kadena uses parallel chains with a braided approach for scalability. Currently Kadena can scale to about 160 tps using 20 parallel chains (about 20 times faster than Bitcoin) in Chainweb. However, with the goal of scaling to over 1000 chains, Kadena could achieve tens of thousands of transactions per second.

Chainweb uses a Petersen Graph (a well-known graph structure in mathematical graph theory) which is a fixed graph structure unlike some other blockchains that use more arbitrary graphs such as a DAG. In the context of

Chainweb, each **vertex** (circle) is a blockchain, and you can see they are all interconnected. This is shown in the following diagram:

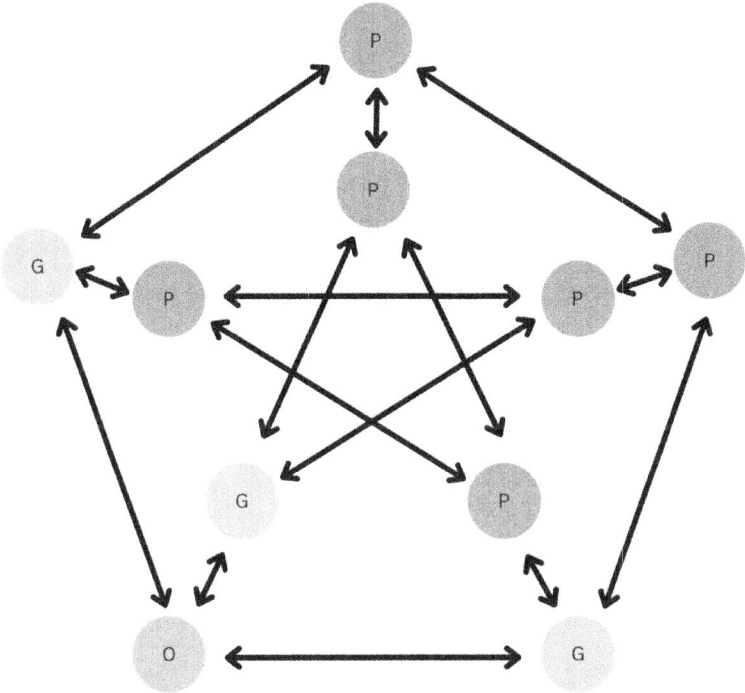

The **orange** blockchain is connected to 3 peers (other blockchains) where it references the block of each of the 3 other chains. Rather than the orange chain pointing to blocks in all other 9 chains, it only needs to point to 3. These are the blockchains in **green**. So, by leveraging graph theory, there are less reference points required. Due to the Petersen Graph structure, each of these green chains then point to 3 other chains (the **purple** chains) and now all 10 blockchains are connected. This is all for the current block height (or point in time).

There are 3 important properties of a Petersen Graph that will help you understand how Chainweb works:

The **Order** is the number of vertices, where each vertex (circle) is a blockchain. In the graph above this is 10 blockchains.

The **Degree** is the number of previous headers of peers a given chain must reference. The edges of the vertex are the specific peers.

The **Diameter** is the maximum number of hops needed to construct a merkle proof between a pair of chains. In more simple terms, it's the maximum number of inter-chain hops required for the chains to be fully connected as per the Petersen Graph structure.

The following shows a blockchain when operating as 1 chain (like Bitcoin) at different block heights. This classic structure is where a block points to the previous block in its own chain (because there is only one chain):

This structure has a Degree of 0 because there are no other peer chains to connect to.

For a braided chain at different block heights (points in time when a block is mined), it's more challenging to illustrate. However, think of each block height as a **layer**. A layer is the set of each chain's block at a given block height. The blockchain in braided form can then be represented in layers where each chain points to previous blocks of other peer chains.

The following shows the Chainweb architecture with 3 **braided** chains (Order 3 and Degree 2). The solid arrows are the connection (pointing to the previous block) of its own chain and the dotted arrows are the connection (pointing to the previous block) to its peer chains:

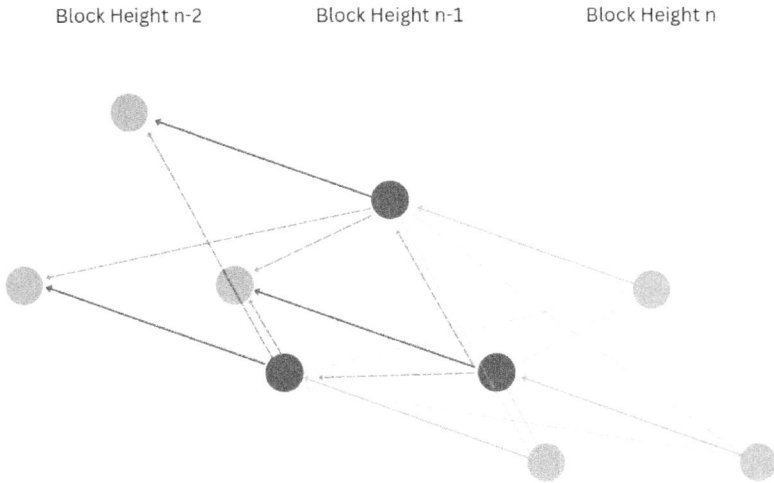

As an analogy, think of braiding like braiding somebody's hair where the strands of hair are interwoven together. In this structure we have 3 blockchains braided together where they are all inter-connected.

So, this shows 3 chains where they are all inter-connected. Each vertex shown by the circle is a chain. Each layer is the previous block, where all 3 chains contain a reference (called the merkle root) to the previous block of its peer chains in a braided approach.

If you have trouble visualizing this, think of a simple graph where the y-axis is the instance of a blockchain (the set of blocks at a point in time), and the x-axis is time (being the blocks that are mined), more specifically called the block height.

The following shows the Chainweb architecture with 10 chains:

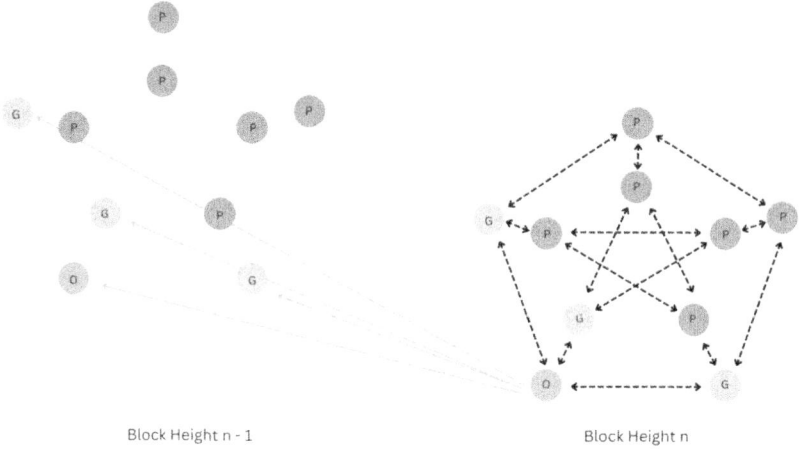

Block Height n - 1   Block Height n

For a given layer you have 10 chains all with their own mined blocks at the current latest block height. Upon the next block being mined (this is the next layer), that next (block height + 1) block then references the past blocks of its peers in addition to the past block of its own chain. For a given block at a block height, n, its past is at block height n-1 and its future is n+1.

Therefore, the diagram shows an Order 10 (10 chains), Degree 3 (points to 3 previous headers of blocks of peers) and Diameter 2 (needs 2 hops to generate a valid merkle proof between a pair of chains). With a degree of 3, this means that only 3 additional references (merkle roots) are required per block. The **orange** chain points to 3 other peers (the dotted orange arrow) and to the previous header of the block for its own chain (the solid orange arrow). For the sake of simplicity only the orange chain is depicted, but in reality, the green chains would point to their previous block headers with dotted green arrows for other peers and a solid green arrow for its own chain, and likewise for the purple chains. You can see the image would get cluttered very quickly if these were included!

In summary, to scale to more chains requires increasing the diameter and degree. For example, with a degree of 7 and diameter 7 it could scale to over 50,000 chains!

From a security perspective, it is now quite clear to see that Kadena is attack resistant since an attacker must essentially fork all blockchains in the network! This is because to replace a block, the attacker must fork all chains that reference the block, either directly or indirectly. Once full coverage has completed, being all chains reference a block directly or indirectly, the attacker must fork all the chains.

From a scalability and useability perspective, Kadena handles congestion by distributing the load among many different chains. When one chain gets congested, more chains can be instantiated, for example growing from 10 to 20 chains in a Chainweb structure of interconnectivity. Users can set up accounts on lower loaded chains, where transaction costs are lower, then transfer their tokens across chains using **Simple Payment Verification** (SPV). This uses a merkle proof which is a cryptographic proof that allows a user to verify that a transaction is included in a block without having to download the entire chain. This is very important for managing cross-chain transfers (more detail on this in the next section).

Managing cross-chain transfers

Managing transfer of cryptocurrency across different chains has been a challenge. Although there are many ways to do it including atomic swaps and "pegging" with bridges (between 2 different chains) there are issues with these approaches. Atomic swap transfers are complicated, and pegging can be subject to hacks due to bridge hacks for example. Pegging involves a token on the destination chain being minted 1:1 relative to the token on the source chain (the source token being burned or locked in the meantime). The problem with pegging is that if there is a hack, the user could end up with the new "artificial token" that was minted and not the native one because they may not be able to redeem the source native token if the hack results in a de-peg of the currency.

Kadena instead allows a single currency to move across its different chains where the token is burned on one chain and minted on the other. The token is always the native token, therefore there is no need to create a new token that is pegged 1:1 with a source token. This works by having SPV proofs of the token that was removed on one chain to be validated by the creation chain. This is done in the application layer.

A Proof of Concept – The Kadena Hybrid Platform

The Kadena Hybrid Platform was just a proof of concept and so has not been rolled out as part of its production mainnet. This was mainly to demonstrate the capability that Kadena can scale to. It also highlights Kadena's level of innovation and experimentation, whereby they are always willing to push the boundaries or abort certain concepts.

With Kadena in this hybrid mode it could achieve up to 480,000 theoretical tps arising from 20 chains connected to 2 Kuro chains (at layer 2) where each Kuro chain achieves 8,000 tps.

A hybrid platform allows public and private blockchain networks to share data between them through smart contracts deployed on each network via a bridge.

A **public blockchain** is also known as a permissionless chain where anyone can contribute. The problems, however, such as GDPR principles for privacy called the "right to be forgotten". This is not possible with an immutable ledger. There is also the issue of slower speeds as many blockchains are challenged with scalability due to the trade-offs with the trilemma.

A **private blockchain**, also known as a permissioned chain, allows users to selectively share data with other participants. The advantages are more privacy and control of how data is shared, faster speeds and more control as to who can engage with the network.

As a final note, let's be clear that they also have their own issues. Some are not even blockchains and the code is closed source. This is where a hybrid solution combining the best of both is considered.

In the context of Kadena, the following are the steps that occur:

- A user posts data to a smart contract on Kadena's public chain.
- This transaction is processed by a bridge between the public and private networks.

- The bridge calls the related smart contract code on the private chain to process the transaction.

This is illustrated in the diagram below:

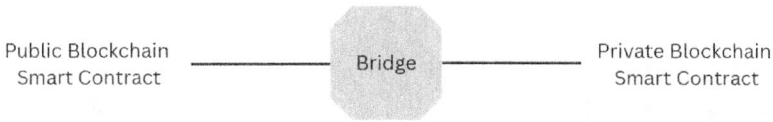

Public Blockchain ——————— Bridge ——————— Private Blockchain
Smart Contract   Smart Contract

One such real world example is JP Morgan who have their own private tokens, but the value of their token can only be redeemed within the company. Therefore, to obtain more revenue, they can leverage a public blockchain where the Hybrid solution allows consumers to access more liquidity as their funds are less restricted, such as on a corporate gift card.

In summary, the hybrid blockchain solution with Kuro allows benefits such as inclusion of liquidity and market access of the public blockchains, Kadena, together with the privacy benefits of the private blockchain, Kuro.

Pact Programming Language

Pact is a smart contract programming language created by Kadena. This book wasn't intended to go to the deeper level of software development, but the reason for describing Pact is that it has some interesting features, namely Formal Verification and Turing Incompleteness.

Turing Incompleteness means there is no unbounded looping or recursion which in smart contracts would be very dangerous. One issue with software development in general is that writing code that contains loops could result in a state where that loop runs infinitely, and the logic never exits the loop, therefore, the code is stuck! In smart contracts especially, this would be dangerous, given that much of the logic involves critical code for finance. Any recursion logic gets detected by Pact and fails immediately.

Formal Verification in Kadena uses a tool suite from Microsoft's Z3 tool and is the ability for the code to formally verify and detect bugs. This system is the same as that used to protect mission critical environments and space autopilot systems. This increases the security of the code and the Kadena ecosystem.

The Pact code is also human readable, and the smart contracts are upgradeable. Upgradable smart contracts as a feature have been quite rare until recently.

Kadena Gas Stations

Kadena uses a novel concept of Gas Stations whereby with certain types of transactions the gas paid by users of the network is essentially free as it's subsidized by corporations and enterprises that build the DApps. An interesting idea! This also encourages users to use the DApps which helps bring adoption and revenue for any company or entity that builds on Kadena.

One such type of gas station is a **Gas Guard** station. This solves the problem where a user wants to move coins from one chain to another, but this requires two gas payments, one on the source chain and one on the destination chain. What if the user doesn't have tokens on the destination chain to pay for gas? The result is that the transaction cannot be completed until there are funds available. Kadena has deployed a gas station with a gas guard to solve this whereby the transaction's gas limit needs to fall within a certain threshold. For an inter-chain transfer to be completed on the destination chain it uses less gas compared to all other transfer functions. A standard transfer function uses a certain amount of gas, but the gas limit guard configures an amount that is less than this. However, it's enough so that an inter-chain transfer can occur. There is an approved function and only this can satisfy the guard for this gas station. All other types of transfers will be above the threshold and fail.

The second type of gas station is a **Gas Payer** station where only certain functions can be called and is only allowed for approved accounts.

So, in summary, gas is subsidized for certain transaction types. Other types of transactions will still require gas to be paid.

Tokenomics

The Kadena token allocations are the following:

- Miners 70%
- Platform 20%, used for funding activities for growing the network and used for gas station grants, insurance and smart contract verification.
- Investors 7%
- Contributors 3% allocated to employees, consultants and advisors.

Miners receive rewards for validating and producing blocks. The block reward is the platform's native currency, KDA. Miners can also receive KDA as fees when transactions are executed on the network. Block rewards are readjusted over time. The block reward began at about 2.3 KDA per block but will decrease by about 0.3% every 87,600 block heights until block height 95,308,800. This is where the mining reward stabilizes at 1 KDA per block. The block reward will eventually drop to zero at block height 125,538,057. Kadena has a fixed quantity of 1 billion tokens, and therefore is mineable for about 120 years. This means Kadena has a disinflationary model where the number of coins coming into circulation over time decreases.

Note that there are token emissions (70% from mining) and platform emissions. The platform emissions are from pre-allocated tokens from launch, and this has an emissions schedule of 10 years, to be completed by 2030.

References

More information on Kadena can be found in the following references:

Community, Ecosystem and Team information:

https://kadena.io/

Documents about Kadena high-level introduction, Chainweb and whitepaper

https://docs.kadena.io/

Latest Developments and News:

https://docs.kadena.io/blogchain

More information on Pact can be found here:

https://docs.kadena.io/pact/beginner

Kaspa

Brief History

Kaspa is a layer 1 platform that aims to solve the blockchain trilemma of achieving scalability and security while maintaining decentralization. It was created by Yonatan Sompolinsky and Aviv Zohar in 2016. The platform uses a Direct Acyclic Graph (DAG) like what Hedera HashGraph uses, but with a Proof-of-Work consensus mechanism like Bitcoin. It was launched in November 2021 and has gained a lot of attention since.

What Problem is Kaspa Solving?

Kaspa is not a Nakamoto consensus but a generalization of it, and it works on a proposal from 2017 to develop into a separate PoW based cryptocurrency and try to push the limits of Nakamoto's consensus from the outside while keeping the generalization in mind.

One of the challenges is orphaned blocks, and Kaspa solves this by allowing orphaned blocks to exist in parallel and order them in consensus unlike Bitcoin. This ensures higher scalability (one block per second compared to Bitcoin's one block per 10 minutes) and security.

The goal of the generalization is to preserve the key aspects of the Nakamoto consensus security-wise while allowing for more scaling.

Bitcoin uses a linear structure of blocks where each block is connected to the previous block, but Kaspa uses a DAG (Directed Acyclic Graph) which is a mathematical structure with directed edges and no cycles, allowing blocks to be connected to many parent blocks.

Orphaned Blocks

Before we delve into the need for a DAG and why it achieves higher scalability, let's first understand what orphaned blocks are and why a BlockDAG helps to resolve the issue of orphaned blocks.

Orphaned blocks can commonly occur in blockchain technologies, and this can severely impact the security of the chain. When a miner discovers a new block, it is first broadcast to the network, and other miners validate it. However, if two miners discover new blocks at the same time, a fork occurs, and the network splits into two chains. This can lead to the creation of orphaned blocks, which are blocks that are not included in the main blockchain.

The following depicts a main chain that has forked into 2 chains where the block in the other chain is now an orphan:

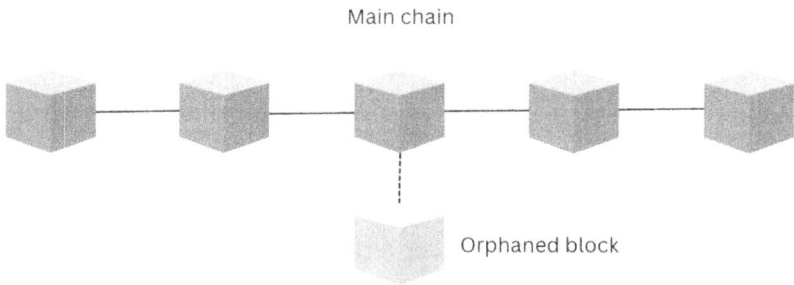

Main chain

Orphaned block

Why orphaned blocks compromise scalability

Orphaned blocks can slow down a blockchain because they are blocks that have been mined simultaneously as another block but not accepted by the blockchain. When two blocks are mined from the same parent block simultaneously, there are two child blocks. Only one of them can be integrated into the chain. The network nodes, which validate blocks, decide which block to use by allowing a small fork between the two child blocks. Then, the nodes determine what block they want to accept by reaching a validation consensus. Each block will have subsequent blocks created, initiating a race to verify the most blocks. The fork with more verified blocks through proof of work (PoW) gets accepted into the blockchain. Any verified blocks within the shorter chain

101

are discarded. The discarded block is called an orphaned block. Any blocks generated from the orphaned block go back to the memory pool to be validated and added to the new chain. This process can slow down the blockchain because it takes time for the network to reach a consensus on which block to accept.

Why orphaned blocks compromise security

Orphaned blocks are a problem because they can create inconsistencies and issues in the blockchain, making it difficult for miners to reach consensus. This can lead to various security issues, including double-spending attacks, which can result in financial losses for users. Also, orphaned blocks can make the network less efficient because miners need to waste resources on blocks that are not ultimately included in the blockchain.

The reason why orphaned blocks compromise security is the following:

- Orphaned blocks reduce the length of the blockchain, making it less secure. A shorter chain makes it easier for attackers to perform a 51% attack. This is a situation where an attacker gains control of most of the network's computing power.
- Orphaned blocks can delay the confirmation of transactions, which makes it difficult for users to know whether their transactions have been successfully processed.
- Due to the waste of resources mining blocks that are not included in the blockchain, orphaned blocks can reduce the rewards earned by miners.

In summary, Proof of Work relies on computing power to secure the network. An orphaned block means the work is wasted so that work isn't used to secure the network. Hence, if there are many orphaned blocks, the network is less secure because less work is used to secure the network.

Architecture and DAG illustration

A DAG (Directed Acyclic Graph) is a data structure that is used to represent a set of objects, where some objects may depend on others. In the context of blockchain, a DAG is a type of data structure that is used to store transactions. Unlike traditional blockchains, where transactions are stored in blocks, a DAG stores transactions in a graph-like structure. Each transaction in a DAG references one or more previous transactions, forming a directed acyclic graph. IOTA chain for example, organizes transactions using a DAG and is not block based. Some DAGs are transaction based without a block structure and other DAGs are block based, being organized as a BlockDAG.

Kaspa is a blockchain network that uses a BlockDAG (Block Directed Acyclic Graph) structure, which allows multiple blocks to coexist in parallel, addressing the issue of blockchain's high orphan rate (where, for instance, two blocks are mined simultaneously, but the network only accepts one of them). Instead of being a single chain like in most crypto projects, Kaspa leverages a DAG, where a block points to several blocks instead of one. The DAG is arranged in a crisscrossed chain, and transactions that align with previous transactions are integrated.

Note in the following diagram that blocks are not in a linear fashion like Bitcoin, they are arranged in parallel where one block can point to more than one parent.

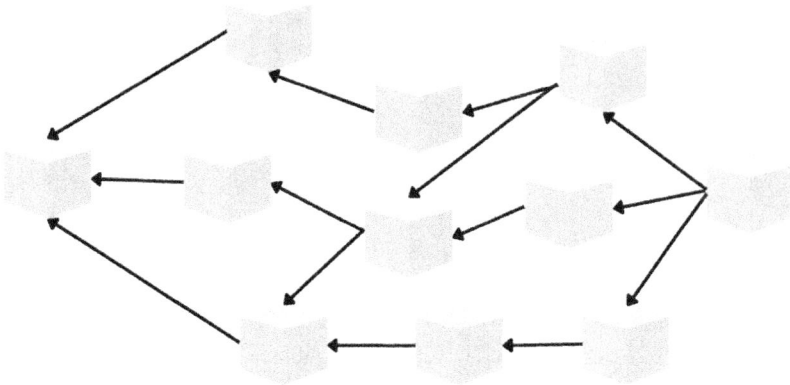

From PHANTOM to GHOSTDAG

Initially, Kaspa implemented the PHANTOM protocol, which required solving an NP-hard problem. To simplify things, NP-complete is a problem that is tough to solve, but easy to verify if a solution is correct. But NP-hard are problems that are ridiculously hard to solve, and, even if someone gave you the answer, it's ridiculously hard to verify if they're correct. To avoid this prohibitive computation, Kaspa devised an efficient greedy algorithm called GHOSTDAG that captures the essence of PHANTOM. GHOSTDAG is the consensus mechanism that Kaspa currently utilizes, and it improves upon the PHANTOM consensus. It uses what is known as a "greedy algorithm" to sort data, and then put each datum in its allocated location.

Let's explore this in more detail. The core idea is that all honest blocks should be well connected in some way. All honest miners should have a well-connected DAG because they are not withholding blocks. An attacker though, would appear quite disconnected from the DAG. But what does well-connected really mean?

First let's understand what a k-cluster is. A k-cluster is a subset of blocks such that every block in it is connected to every block in it, apart from at most k blocks. This example below is a 2-cluster. The algorithm will decide what the most optimal cluster level is (for example 2-cluster, 3-cluster, etc).

The following helps to illustrate this using a 2-cluster:

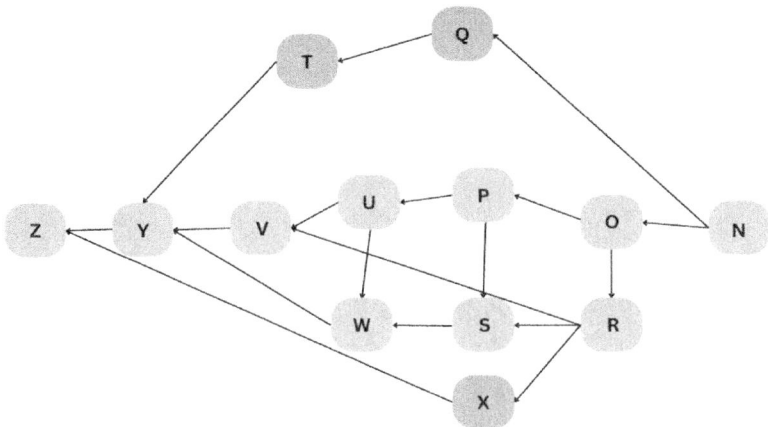

Given a block Y, its past is the set of blocks which are reachable from Y, in this case Z. Its future is the set of all blocks Y is reachable from. All other blocks are called its anticone. Blocks part of its anticone are not directly part of its past or future. Block R for example, has blocks P and U as part of its anticone, but this is not more than k (which is 2) so this is part of the well-connected set.

You can see that V is not connected to W and S, and U is not connected to S and R. Again, that is ok because it's no more than k. This is a 2-cluster. A k-cluster in a DAG is a subset with the property that no block in the subset has an anticone larger than k. In this case Q has an anticone larger than k. It is not well-connected (not connected to V,U,P,O,W,S,R). The same goes for T and X. Therefore, you can see that X, Q and T are not well-connected. A well-connected block needs to be connected to every other block apart from at most k blocks.

Essentially the summary is to find the biggest sub-DAG where no block has an anticone greater than k. This is a generalization of the Bitcoin longest chain rule, where Bitcoin can be described as PHANTOM with k=0.

If this is heavy to understand, then without getting into too much detail you can see from the naked eye that essentially the nodes in red do look somewhat disconnected with respect to those in blue. Also, dishonest blocks tend to be only connected to old blocks and never to new ones.

So, PHANTOM has an ordering mechanism across all blocks in 3 steps as per the following:

- It recognizes a set of well-connected blocks (known as the blue set) and uses this as a base to exclude malicious blocks that are not well-connected (known as the red set). An example of blocks in the red set would be those that only ever point to old blocks.
- The DAGs order is completed by favoring blocks inside the cluster (k-cluster) and penalizing those outside it (the red set).
- The ordering of the blocks gives rise to the order of the transactions to make sure that a consistency for all approved transactions is maintained.

In summary, unlike Bitcoin where blocks not on the main chain are discarded, PHANTOM includes all blocks in the BlockDAG in the ledger, but places those by attackers later. So those blocks marked as blue (well-connected honest) are included and ordered in the ledger, but those in red (or not well-connected malicious) are still part of the ledger but are ordered much later and penalized.

However, there are issues with PHANTOM that GHOSTDAG can solve. This is the following:

- It could not be implemented efficiently because the problem of finding a maximal k-cluster is very difficult.
- The entire computation must be restarted each time the DAG updates, and this requires storing the entire DAG structure.

GHOSTDAG is a greedy variant of PHANTOM that addresses these issues because the k-cluster is maintained incrementally. Each block has a number called its blue score. This reveals how many blocks in its past are in the k-cluster. For a certain block, it chooses the parent with the highest blue score. When a new block is created, the algorithm doesn't need to calculate the entire k-cluster in the DAG because it inherits most of the k-cluster from its selected parent.

DAGKnight

This is a new enhancement to GHOSTDAG with the goal of making Kaspa resistant to 51% attacks.

A 51% attack occurs when a group owns more than 50% of the nodes on the network, allowing the controlling parties to alter the blockchain. Now, if latency increases suddenly, this increases the likelihood of attack because now one needs a lower percentage of ownership to start an attack. To resolve this issue currently, blockchains sacrifice block confirmation time by setting an assumed network delay parameter.

However, with the DAGKnight enhancement it actively analyses and responds to the network conditions in real time and adjusts block confirmation times dynamically based on the health of the network rather than using an assumed network delay.

Kaspa Pruning

Pruning is a process that refers to the automatic deletion of outdated or excessive data. In the context of blockchain, pruning is used to reduce the size of the BlockDAG structure, which helps nodes to store only necessary data, and not have to keep track of large amounts of information.

Kaspa has implemented a new pruning mechanism that happens 'on-the-fly'. This means that the pruning process is continuous and automatic, without any need to pause or restart the system. Kaspa nodes only need about 3 days of history meaning that many nodes can be run without large storage requirements.

Kaspa Mining

This book assumes some knowledge on mining and the process is explained in more detail in the Bitcoin section and the Proof of Work section at the beginning of this book. However, Kaspa mining uses a modified version of PoW called KHeavyHash which is designed to be more energy efficient than Bitcoin's SHA 256 algorithm.

It's possible to mine Kaspa on a PC using a GPU. However, the efficiency and profitability will be significantly lower compared to using specialized mining hardware like ASICs. Just like Bitcoin, miners in Kaspa can choose solo mining or join mining pools.

The GHOSTDAG protocol gives a significant advantage to miners by allowing multiple blocks to exist in parallel.

Tokenomics

Kaspa's token, KAS, had a fair launch in November 2021 with no pre-mine, zero pre-sales, and no coin allocations. The maximum supply of KAS is 28.7 billion coins, and the current circulating supply is approximately 21.59 billion KAS. The emission schedule halves once per year (compared to Bitcoin's halving every 4 years) via smooth monthly reductions by a factor of $(1/2)^{(1/12)}$.

Therefore, Kaspa is a disinflationary coin meaning that the inflation reduces over time just like Bitcoin. Given that it also has the upper limit, this creates scarcity which appears to be a positive approach given the success of Bitcoin's tokenomics.

References

The following references contain more detail from a technical and ecosystem perspective to expand your knowledge:

PHANTOM GHOSTDAG whitepaper:

https://eprint.iacr.org/2018/104.pdf

Kaspa website with resources, features, developments and latest news:

https://kaspa.org/

Proof of Stake Chains

Ethereum

Brief History

Ethereum was proposed in late 2013 by Vitalik Buterin and it was later developed by a team of developers, including Buterin, and officially launched on July 30, 2015. Ethereum is renowned for introducing smart contracts, which are self-executing contracts and largely this allows decentralized applications (DApps) to be built on it.

Ethereum introduced its native cryptocurrency called ETH which serves multiple purposes including gas for transactions, serving as a means of value transfer and powering smart contracts. Its main innovation is smart contracts, which enable the execution of programmable code, requiring no need for middlemen. This allows automation and transparency in various applications, such as decentralized finance (DeFi), gaming and supply chain for example.

Ethereum introduced the ERC-20 token standard, which became the foundation for most tokens issued on its blockchain. These are fungible tokens that are bound by a set of rules, which facilitates tradability and interoperability with other tokens and platforms.

As a result of its success, there was a rise of Initial Coin Offerings (ICOs), which is an approach to raise funds where projects issue tokens on the Ethereum blockchain in exchange for ETH or other cryptocurrencies.

It has faced scalability challenges due to network congestion and therefore high transaction fees when demand is high. To help address this, Ethereum has had many network upgrades, the main one being Ethereum 2.0, which was a transition from a PoW to PoS consensus which in turn also aids energy efficiency.

The tokenomics and smart contract functionality have made it a leading blockchain platform resulting in huge adoption.

What Problem is Ethereum trying to solve?

Ethereum aimed to solve problems that Bitcoin couldn't address effectively. While Bitcoin introduced the concept of a decentralized digital currency and blockchain technology, which is a huge innovation, Ethereum looked to expand upon this by focusing on programmability and flexibility, and effectively to some, becoming a "world supercomputer". Here are some of the problems that Ethereum aimed to solve:

Customization and Versatility:

Ethereum's architecture allows more versatility and customization compared to Bitcoin. Bitcoin was mainly designed for peer-to-peer electronic cash transactions and more recently a store of value. However, Ethereum allowed for the creation of many DApps beyond transfer of tokens or simply being a store of value. For example, smart contracts can represent many different styles of agreements, from financial derivatives to token issuance, voting systems and decentralized autonomous organizations (DAOs).

Smart Contracts:

Bitcoin's scripting language is not very flexible and focused on transaction functionality. There was no support for complex smart contracts or DApps. Ethereum introduced a Turing-complete scripting language, thus allowing the creation and execution of arbitrary code on the blockchain. This programmability gave rise to the development of a huge variety of DApps, being financial instruments, decentralized exchanges (DEXs) and games for example.

A Token Standard:

Ethereum introduced the ERC-20 token standard, which allowed creation and interoperability of tokens on the Ethereum blockchain, which Bitcoin's scripting language doesn't support to the same extent. This enabled the proliferation of ICOs that provided a new way for startups to raise capital.

Scalability and Governance:

While it is known that Ethereum and Bitcoin faced scalability issues, Ethereum had an approach to governance and network upgrades that facilitated more innovation and adaptability.

Ethereum's community-driven governance model and ability to implement protocol upgrades through hard forks allowed for improvements in scalability, security, and more features.

In summary, it could be argued that these were not all problems that Bitcoin was not able to solve as such. Many in the Bitcoin community would say it was never intended for all these issues to be addressed as it was not part of the Bitcoin vision or design in the first place. Rather, Ethereum took a completely different approach and looked to solve problems in general with the financial system for example, among others. Ethereum and Bitcoin are a different beast altogether, some would say. Bitcoin is primarily a store of value, much like digital gold and Ethereum, while it may have a portion of that narrative, is more a flexible world supercomputer with support for DApps. However, the concrete definition for Ethereum is very debatable in the wider community, but it could be said that this is its strength in that no label or attempt to classify it allows a more open-minded approach and innovation going forward.

Proof of Stake in Ethereum

The move from PoW to PoS was a large upgrade known as The Merge (part of Ethereum's roadmap) and sought to achieve energy efficiency and scalability among others.

As a requirement, validators need to stake 32 ETH in a smart contract. Note that staking more than 32 ETH per validator gains no advantage over others. If a user wants to stake more, they can set up separate validators.

However, not every node in Ethereum must be a validator. There are different node types in Ethereum.

Full Nodes validate the blockchain block by block and this can be done from genesis or from a more recent block, so there are different types of full nodes. However, they only maintain a copy of recent data, and old data is deleted to save disk space, but it can be generated again when required. Typically, a validator runs as a full node.

Archival Nodes store the full history of the blockchain where this is useful for audits, research and analysis, but due to the large disk space requirements it's not recommended that validators run as an archival node. These nodes are useful for when a user wants to query an account balance for a given block number or make any search queries in a block explorer at any point in the chain's history. The query times are relatively slow due to the extensive search required and this is another reason why validators don't run in this mode.

Light Nodes run a less heavyweight version by only downloading block headers from the chain and this enables users to set up Ethereum nodes without the high hardware requirements and thus could eventually be used on mobile devices for example. They don't partake in consensus but are able to perform a level of verification of the data received.

It is also important to describe another vital part of Ethereum known as the **Ethereum Virtual Machine (EVM).** The EVM is a piece of software that runs on an Ethereum node and serves as the main heart of the Ethereum network where it behaves as a decentralized, Turing-complete virtual machine and provides the runtime environment for executing smart contracts. Ethereum operates as a distributed state machine and the EVM manages that state, such as smart contract code, accounts and the machine state, which can change from block to block based on certain rules. For example, when a new block is created and linked to the blockchain, the state machine processes the block whereby there is a state transition from the previous state of that block to the new state.

The following illustrates the EVM and its role in the Ethereum network:

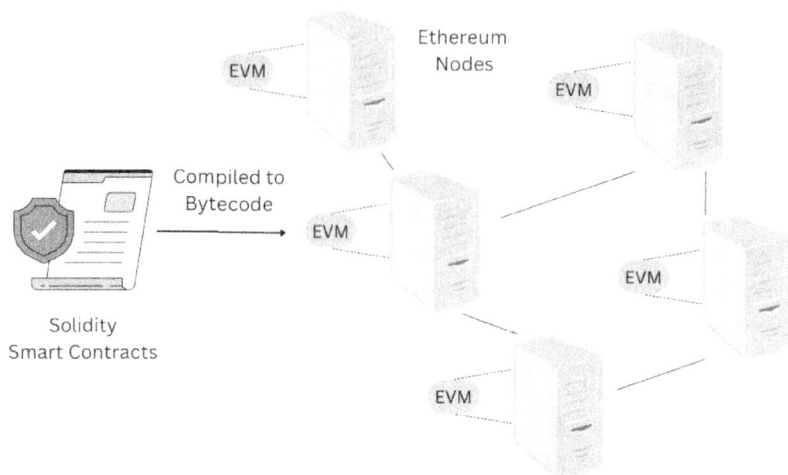

Smart contract code is written in a language called Solidity and then compiled into something called Bytecode that the EVM understands. These are low level instructions that the EVM executes to run smart contracts.

Now that the fundamentals of node types and the EVM have been described, this lays the platform for describing Proof of Stake. The following describes how Proof of Stake in Ethereum works and the role of Validators step by step:

Prerequisites for a Validator:

In addition to 32 ETH being deposited, the user must run three main pieces of software:

- **Execution client**. This handles execution of transactions and smart contracts and checks to make sure the transaction is correctly signed. It then adds the transaction to its local mempool and broadcasts it to the network. This client runs the EVM, where the transactions are executed in the EVM, and it holds the current state and storage of all Ethereum data.

- **Consensus client**. This manages consensus rules and connects to other nodes and receives validated data from execution clients, which enables the network to achieve agreement. It also manages penalties for misbehavior. This client does not vote on any blocks, but rather aggregates these attestations from validators to decipher if the block is valid. It also selects a validator to propose new blocks and then sends that proposal to the execution client for validation.
- **Validator client**. This allows the node to validate blocks and secure the network, which means building and proposing blocks when selected and voting on blocks they receive on the network.

The Validator then needs to join an activation queue, which restricts the rate of new validators joining the network to ensure stability of the validator set.

Note that a standard Ethereum node only needs to run the Execution client and Consensus client. The Validator client is only required to be an actual validator.

Executing a Transaction:

- A user initiates a transaction and creates and signs the transaction with their private key.
- The transaction is submitted to an execution client.
- The execution client verifies its validity.
- If valid, the transaction is added to the local mempool and broadcasted to other nodes.

Voting (also known as **Attestations**):

Ethereum operates in slots (each lasting 12 seconds) and epochs (comprising 32 slots, which is about 6.4 minutes). The full validator set is all the validators in the system. However, there is a group of at least 128 validators randomly selected for each slot within the epoch to form a committee, so that's 32 committees per epoch. Note that there are many committees per slot, and the number increases with the size of the validator set. A validator can only be part of the committee once per epoch. Then the next epoch there is a rotation whereby new validators in the queue are selected as part of a new committee for each slot. This is to enhance security and prevent collusion.

- For each slot, a validator is randomly selected as the block proposer.
- This proposer creates a new block and sends it to other nodes.
- The committee of validators validates the proposed block.
- Validators in the committee receive new blocks from peers. Note that all other validators also receive these blocks but don't partake in the voting process.
- The committee validators re-execute transactions in the block to validate state changes. To maintain consistency all other validators also do the same so that they can include the block in their database.
- The validators in the committee send a vote in favor of the block.
- The committee votes determine whether the block is valid and if 2/3 of the votes (the supermajority) approve then the block is accepted.

If a block is not accepted for a slot (that is more than 1/3 of votes do not accept it) the block is discarded and a new block is proposed. Given that there are 32 slots per epoch this provides the potential for 32 blocks to be accepted and added to the chain for that epoch.

Slashing and Penalties:

If a validator behaves dishonestly, for example by proposing multiple conflicting blocks, their staked ETH can be slashed.

- Double voting also leads to slashing.
- The severity of slashing depends on the violation.
- The deactivation period is anything from 18 hours to 18 days depending on the severity of the issue.
- If a validator is slashed, it doesn't mean they cannot validate again, but rather now that they have less ETH, they are put much deeper into the queue for the validator set. That validator can then top up back to 32 ETH to progress further in the queue should it wish to.

Note that the Validator in this section that gets selected to propose a block is also known as a block proposer. The Proposer role is very important and is mentioned in the "MEV in Ethereum" section.

ETH issuance

The issuance is the ETH reward to stakers because of processing transactions for a newly created block. Since the advent of PoS, Ethereum's issuance has decreased dramatically. This reduction assisted in making ETH scarcer in that in PoW the issuance was about 90% higher. The annual inflation rate for Ethereum dropped from 4.5% to about 0.43%, although this is changing all the time. Before the move to PoS, miners were issued about 13000 ETH per day, but this dropped to about 1700 ETH per day after the move. Due to a high number of transactions on Ethereum soon after the move to PoS it became net deflationary. This is because a portion of ETH is burned with each transaction, and there was more ETH burned than was being produced (or issued) by the protocol.

The two approaches to maintain a security budget for the network are issuance and transaction fees. However, if issuance is too high, it will dilute ETH as an asset, essentially resulting in inflation. On the contrary, if issuance is insufficient, this could result in network attacks as there is less incentive to keep the validators honest.

Ethereum's solution was to designate a base issuance to scale the security in relation to the total staked ETH on the network. The model is a little like a varying minimum wage that is affected by the total amount of ETH staked (which is essentially related to the number of validators). With a lower amount of ETH staked, this increases the chance of attacks, so this means more financial incentives are needed to bring validators into the system. In this scenario the reward, being the base issuance, is increased. The reverse is true when more validators come online because this increases security. Now that the network is more secure, the base issuance is correspondingly decreased (this also benefits ETH holders because the network operates with a lower inflation rate). Therefore, the more validators that connect to the Ethereum network, the lower the base reward per validator. There is a formula to calculate this, but in summary the base issuance per validator is inversely proportional to the square root of the total amount of staked ETH on the network.

Transaction Fees and EIP-1559

There was a change to the gas fee structure before the move to PoS whereby a new Ethereum Improvement Proposal (EIP) was implemented. It was not directly related to the move to PoS, but is nonetheless a significant improvement.

The move behind EIP-1559 was to introduce less volatility and more predictability for Ethereum's transaction fees. This was to address problems where users were overpaying for transactions due to gas prices fluctuating up and down.

Previously it used a gas fee model that was auction based, but EIP-1559 introduced a new model where this is a **base fee** and a **priority fee**. The base fee is a fixed fee per block that changes dynamically based on the level of network congestion and the block size can grow or shrink to handle changes in congestion. The priority fee is where users can specify an additional fee (essentially a tip) to incentivize validators to include their transactions as a priority over others.

In addition to this, the improvement also introduced a fee burning mechanism whereby the base fee for each transaction is burned to assist in making ETH more deflationary.

Ethereum Architecture for Block Validation

The following shows the block validation process with respect to epochs. It shows the start of each epoch where each slot is assigned a validator as a block proposer. For each slot, the block proposer selects a block to be linked on to the main chain. The committee then votes to add this to the main chain, where the votes are weighted based on the validator's stake. The votes are then propagated through the network. A block with 2/3 of the majority votes is then added to the chain.

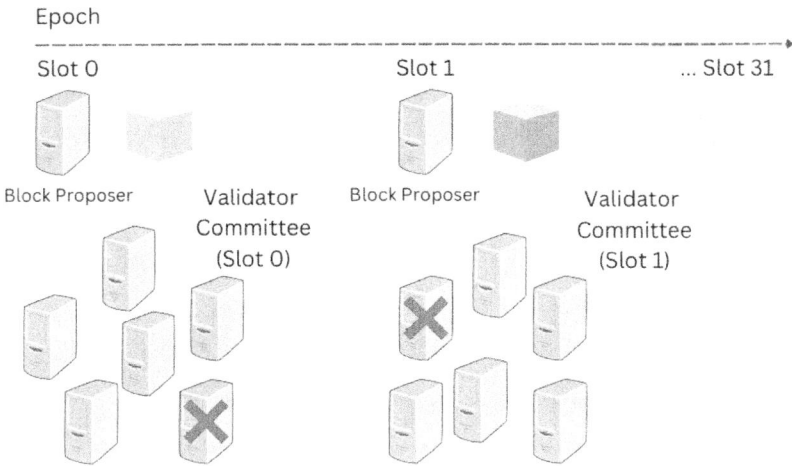

Epoch

Slot 0   Slot 1   ... Slot 31

Block Proposer   Validator   Block Proposer   Validator
Committee   Committee
(Slot 0)   (Slot 1)

MEV in Ethereum

There is a concept in Ethereum called MEV (Maximum Extractable Value) for Validators to extract more value from a block of transactions. Before we delve into this let's review how Ethereum transactions are finalized. Upon using the Ethereum network, users' transactions get inserted into a mempool, which is a pool of pending transactions. After that, validators choose transactions from the mempool which get put in blocks and then get sent to other validators for consensus.

As a reward for this work done, the validators receive tips from the transaction fees and a block reward called the issuance, that being ETH. There is another way to earn rewards and that is in the form of MEV. This is the total value that can be extracted from a block in addition to the standard block reward and gas fees through the excluding and re-ordering of transactions within the block, or frontrunning.

121

How does MEV get extracted?

It's not only validators who profit from MEV. A large amount is also extracted by separate network users called searchers, who scan the mempool for profitable MEV opportunities and then use bots to take advantage of them.

One of the main methods of MEV extraction is called frontrunning which involves **searchers** using frontrunner bots to scan the mempool for profitable transactions. They then submit the same transaction with a higher gas price meaning that the validator will then pick this one first.

There are other methods such as DEX arbitrage, which takes advantage of different prices of the same token on different DEXs, and sandwich attacks.

Advantages and disadvantages of MEV

Many in the community claim there is a centralization risk due to validators looking to make as much profit as possible now that don't perform intensive work like the miners did in the PoW model. Therefore, since the ETH issuance has decreased roughly 90% in block rewards because of the move from PoW to PoS, there is a tendency to look for other opportunities to increase the overall rewards and that one is MEV.

Another problem is the requirement of staking 32 ETH to become a validator, which has led to many staking pools running lot of validators, which in turn has resulted in an increase of resources for MEV extraction potential. Many individual stakers cannot compete and so tend to join these pools to increase profits. This, however, would increase centralization in Ethereum.

Many unethical MEV opportunities are because the mempool is public and so anyone can view Ethereum's pending transactions. It would be more desirable if this could be avoided as this would mitigate frontrunning and remove stiff competition between searchers.

In terms of advantages though, DEX arbitrage can maintain stability for asset prices.

However, it is clear there are many issues arising from MEV but there is a solution. It's called MEV-Boost by Flashbots using a Proposer Builder separation.

Note that MEV-Boost is not inherently related to Ethereum 2.0, but in the meantime has been deemed a suitable solution.

Flashbots and Proposer Builder Separation

One important fundamental with MEV and block production is that the entity that constructs a block cannot be the same entity that proposes that block. In PBS, block builders have the task of creating blocks and block proposers choose the most profitable block without knowing its contents. This leads to 3 advantages:

- It makes it more difficult for block builders to censor transactions. Certain criteria can be included so that no censorship occurs before a block is proposed. Therefore, because the proposer has inclusion lists this protects against builders censoring transactions. If transactions are missing from this list, the proposer can either decline the block or add those missing transactions and then propose the block.
- The responsibilities are better allocated as it means builders and proposers can optimize their tasks, which improves efficiency.
- It helps to prevent centralization as smaller validators (compared to institutional ones) can compete, thus allowing a fairer distribution of rewards.

MEV-Boost by Flashbots essentially outsources the building of blocks to separate entities called builders. It is a piece of open-source middleware designed for validators to access a competitive block building market.

Ethereum 2.0 is looking to implement its own Proposer Builder Separation (PBS) where validators will act as both builders and proposers, but in the meantime Flashbots offers a solution to many of the issues mentioned.

MEV in action step-by-step

In this section it's important to note that Ethereum runs two clients. One is the Execution client to execute transactions, and the other is the Consensus client to reach consensus on a new block that has been created.

The flow of MEV is as per the following:

- **Searchers** identify high value transactions in a block such as high gas fees or arbitrage opportunities. They then submit sealed-price bids allowing privacy of transactions and fairer competition, preventing bidding wars and preventing builders from censoring transactions. This contrasts with a previous approach where a priority gas auction was used.
- The **Builders** then check the proposals from the Searchers and then extract transactions from the mempool to build blocks with high value, based on MEV and transaction fees.
- Builders then send their blocks to a Relay which checks that the blocks are valid and calculates the total value of the data in the block, known as the payload. They aggregate blocks from multiple Builders and select the block with the highest rewards.
- **Relays** act as a trusted entity between Builders and Validators (block Proposers). They send the payload data to an escrow, and just the payload header to Validators.
- An escrow allows data to be available to Validators by guaranteeing the accuracy and validity of transactions without revealing the transactions themselves ensuring security and fairness.
- Validators extract the most profitable block (via the payload header) and send it back to the Relay where it broadcasts it to the network.
- Note that if the Validator proposes a different block, that means they have signed two blocks resulting in a penalty where their ETH is slashed.

Also note that although the Relays are a trusted entity, Flashbots is looking to decentralize their Relays.

The following diagram shows the flow and interaction of builders, searchers and validators for MEV extraction:

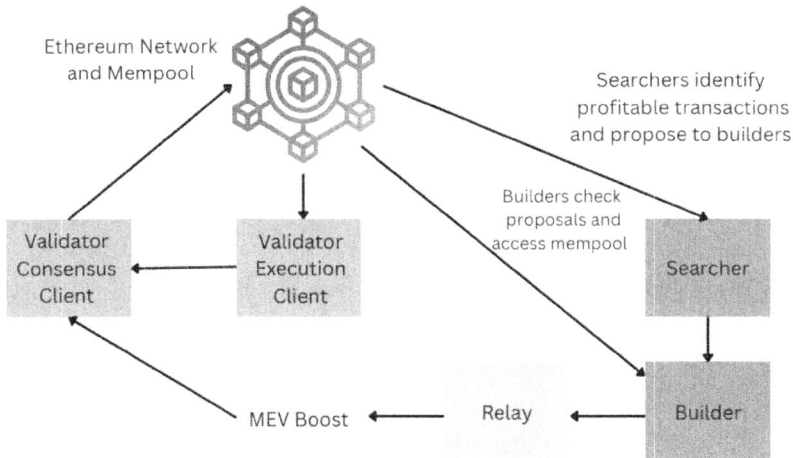

Note that the Builders and Proposers are not necessarily separate nodes as such. The separation is more conceptual than physical. A validator node can switch between roles accordingly and so can participate as a builder to build blocks and as a searcher to identify value and make queries.

Weak Subjectivity in PoS vs the Objective Approach in PoW

This topic is applicable to PoS and PoW in general, but now that Bitcoin and Ethereum as well as PoS and PoW have been described, this is a good point in the book to highlight the subjective approach in PoS compared to the Objective approach in PoW, now that there is more context.

Let's first understand what Objective and Subjective mean in the context of blockchains, then what Weak Subjectivity means.

Objective is where a new node comes online with no knowledge except two things:

- The definition of the protocol
- The set of all blocks and other relevant messages which contain verifiable facts that have been published, and so can independently come to the same conclusion as the rest of the network relating to the current state.

Subjective is where the system has stable states where nodes come to different conclusions, and a lot of information is required to participate and make decisions. Essentially subjectivity is where there can be potentially many versions of a blockchain ledger that appear correct.

Weak Subjectivity is where a new node comes online with no knowledge except three things:

- The definition of the protocol
- The set of all blocks and other relevant messages that have been published
- A state from less than X blocks ago that is known to be valid can come to the same conclusion as the rest of the network on the current state. If an attacker has permanently more than a certain percentage control over the group of nodes involved in consensus then this would compromise the valid state.

In the case of Weak Subjectivity nodes that are always online are ok and so in this case essentially Weak Subjectivity is then equivalent to Objectivity. Nodes that come online occasionally, or at least once in X blocks are fine because they can always get an updated state of the blockchain. However, a new node appearing online or after a long period, doesn't have protection from the consensus mechanism. The solution is to obtain a recent hash of a block from a block explorer or friend and insert it into their client as a checkpoint. In other words, Weak Subjectivity is where subjectivity is unacceptable for short periods, but acceptable for long periods. Therefore, if there is a node that is continuously online, it will be able to automatically determine the correct ledger, but if the node is then offline for months, it may need to get information from another node such as friend that has an online node, or a block explorer, to determine the correct ledger.

Advantages and Disadvantages of Weak Subjectivity

Pros:

- It is possible to mitigate certain types of attacks called **long range attacks**. This is where an attacker tries to create a longer chain than the main one where the goal is to overwrite the history of the chain and reverse transactions or double spend the tokens. If the attacker's longer chain is later revealed, it could invalidate transactions confirmed many blocks ago, which leads to a long range fork. This type of attack is perhaps more possible in PoS because there are not huge amounts of computing power required like in PoW. However, this can be mitigated by checkpoints or the behavioral process of weak subjectivity itself. Therefore, since initial knowledge is required of the recent state it can reject forks that deviate from expectations. In a sense this flexibility can be a positive with respect to the Objective approach.
- Although there is some trust required to sync to a new chain there are ways to mitigate this by using checkpoints. A **checkpoint** is a state that is agreed upon by most of the network as belonging to the canonical chain. A new node can get this checkpoint from a trusted source such as a website, forum or friend.
- The community can resort to social recovery of the honest chain if a 51% attack arises due to the reasons already mentioned.

Cons:

- Long range attacks can still be a threat if not mitigated properly.
- Checkpoints still require some initial trust for a new node to sync to the correct chain and if not done properly there is a risk of syncing to the

wrong history. For example, if over 33% of validators that remove their stake continue to attest and produce blocks, they could produce a different fork, thus conflicting with the main chain. New nodes starting up or have been offline may not know that these validators have removed their stake, so attackers could fool them into using the wrong chain. Checkpoints can mitigate this though. The section on Checkpoints later describes this more.

Advantages and Disadvantages of Objective

Pros:

- Simpler and more intuitive as it relies on a fixed set of rules with no subjectivity.
- It relies on objective facts and evidence of blockchain history.
- Creates high social consensus over time as nodes tend to converge on the same chain, such as in Bitcoin where nodes use the longest chain rule and PoW to determine the valid chain.

Cons:

- It's vulnerable to long range attacks where a secret fork could overtake the chain and unlike the weak subjective approach there is little mitigate this. This is because there is a fixed set of rules to determine the validity of the blockchain state with little flexibility.

Checkpoints

Finality in Ethereum is organized through checkpoint blocks where the first block in each epoch is a checkpoint. Validators vote on which pair of checkpoints are valid, the voting being across two epochs, one checkpoint per epoch. This is called a supermajority link between two checkpoints, and this is when a transaction can be considered finalized, whereby 66% of all the staked ETH agrees on the two checkpoints.

They serve the same purpose as genesis blocks, except that they are not positioned at the genesis of the blockchain. There is a fork choice algorithm that trusts that the blockchain state for that checkpoint is correct and so verifies the chain from that point and into the future. This allows validators to trust the recent history without validating the entire chain from genesis. Therefore, there is a distinct line for the checkpoints meaning that there is no point of reversion because blocks located before checkpoints cannot be altered. This means that long range attacks are rendered useless because the design is such that long range forks are invalid.

New nodes cannot be fooled by invalid forks by validators whose stake has been withdrawn. This is because the checkpoints are separated by a shorter time than the validator withdrawal period, so if a validator forks the chain, it is slashed some ETH before they can withdraw their stake.

The following illustrates checkpoints in that the portion of the chain that has been finalized has no possibility of being reverted, whilst the portion after that checkpoint is still liable to a fork. However, it's clear that this would not be a long-range fork because long range forks are defined as being deep into the history of the chain.

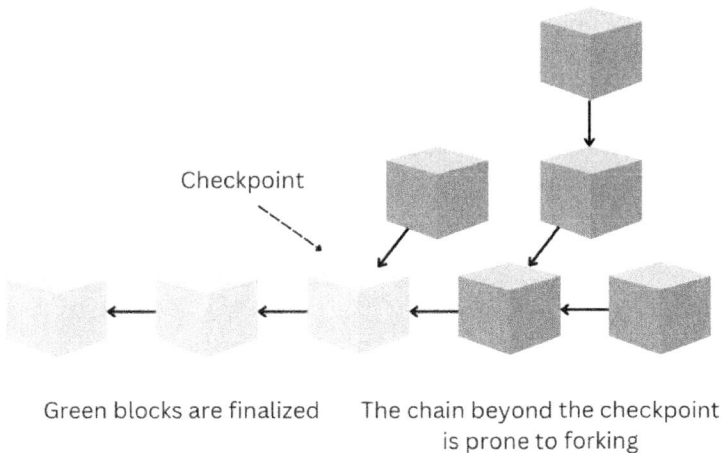

Checkpoint

Green blocks are finalized   The chain beyond the checkpoint
                                   is prone to forking

Weak Subjectivity vs Objective Summary

PoW consensus is a way for nodes to agree on the order of transactions in an objective way without trusting other nodes. PoS is more subjective, albeit weakly subjective. The issue with the weak subjective approach is that if a node is offline, it must trust some node to initially sync up. If it trusts the wrong node it could sync to an alternate history. In PoW as soon as the node sees a node with a larger PoW it will re-org to that state. However, the PoW objective approach can be subject to long range attacks. As the reader, which do you prefer more? Both have their tradeoffs.

Upcoming Updates

Proto danksharding (EIP 4844)

This is an improvement proposal to reduce layer 2 gas fees on Ethereum. Before delving into proto danksharding, it's important to understand why the plan to originally use sharding may not have been the solution to reducing gas fees.

At the present time however, **sharding** is no longer part of the Ethereum roadmap, because the community realized the effectiveness of **layer 2 rollups**, which are off-chain solutions that improve scalability by aggregating transactions and then upload them to the base layer (layer 1), and reducing the load on the base layer, Ethereum itself. These rollups bundle transactions into batches off-chain at layer 2. So, rather than posting each transaction individually, a summary of changes is submitted for the entire batch.

However, sharding enables Ethereum's scalability to be increased by splitting the network into smaller, interconnected shard chains, where each shard handles a subset of transactions and allows parallel processing of transactions. Although sharding could increase scalability, it was then thought that this could lead to a reduction of gas fees, but this may not be the case. This is because it's all about supply and demand in that if the traffic is increased due to high demand, sharding will assist to handle that increase in traffic. However, this means Ethereum trading volume could increase 10 times, but if the ETH price increases by about the same amount, then the gas fees will likely not be reduced. This is just speculation, but it highlights the possibility. The point being there is no guarantee of gas fee reduction. There is a proposed upper limit of 1024 sharded chains where to guarantee security each chain needs to have about 100 nodes to decrease vulnerability. So, at the layer 1 level, we could say there is a scalability limit (due to the 1024 chains limit) and in a sense, a limit to gas fee reduction, but at the layer 2, the sky is the limit because there is no restriction on the amount of layer 2 as such.

It may turn out that layer 1 fees increase due to the demand, whereas scaling at layer 2 provides the opportunity to rectify this where layer 1 fees become more stable, and layer 2 fees decrease due to infinite scaling potential. Without sharding (and therefore taking the focus off scaling at layer 1) this means that layer 1 can focus on security and decentralization, and layer 2 on scaling. The interesting outcome of all this is that eventually all transactions on layer 1 could be from data uploaded from the off-chain layer 2, in turn increasing privacy as there will be no record of individual users or transactions, only batched up transactions from layer 2. This will be even more likely if layer 1 fees increase due to the ETH price increasing.

So, with the pivot away from sharding, a concept known as proto danksharding emerged, involving adding blobs of rollup data to Ethereum blocks, which validators can efficiently verify, which made the need for sharded chains slightly less required. Currently, rollups post their transactions in CALLDATA (a field on the main blockchain) and this puts a limit on how cheap they can make user transactions. It's processed by all Ethereum nodes and resides on chain permanently so makes it more expensive, but rollups only require the data for a short period. The reason for this is rollup data is used to reconstruct and verify the off-chain transactions, which are then compressed and uploaded to the main chain. Once they are verified, the rollup data can be discarded. To keep a record of the verification there is a type of proof called **ZK (zero knowledge) proof**s which can prove correctness of a transaction without revealing details of the computation. These can remain on chain as they are much smaller than rollup data and don't need to be reconstructed and so serve as a historical record for the off-chain (layer 2) transactions.

Proto danksharding introduces data blobs that can be sent and attached to blocks. The data in these blobs is not accessible to the EVM (and thus, execution clients) and is automatically pruned after 1 to 3 months. A rollup has two main parts to it, the data, being the set of transactions, and an execution check, being the re-execution of those transactions to verify the correctness of the proposed state change. For the execution check, the transaction data must be available for a certain period for a node to check it, but it doesn't need to be permanently available. Therefore, rollups can send their data more cost effectively meaning that end users can experience cheaper transactions. So, the nodes hold the blobs of data in the consensus client, and they agree that they have viewed the data, which is later pruned. If the data was stored permanently, these clients would suffer from huge storage bloat increasing hardware costs.

Eventually also, something called full danksharding will be implemented to reduce rollup costs even further. This will increase the number of blobs attached to blocks from 1 in proto danksharding to 64 in full danksharding.

Tokenomics

In 2014, Ethereum conducted an ICO that later became a precedent for following token ICOs on Ethereum. The native token, ETH, was sold by Ethereum developers to investors and raised over $18 million. Investors exchanged BTC for ETH where on the first day about 7 million ETH were sold and eventually the ICO sold over 50 million ETH.

Since the move to PoS the base fees (through EIP-1559) are burned for each transaction and with increased demand, this creates a deflationary effect if more ETH is burned than is issued. Note that also the act of validators staking tokens means that essentially tokens are removed from the circulating supply for that period which also increases the scarcity.

The use cases of the coin are for gas fees for transactions and executing smart contracts, validators staking ETH to earn rewards and assist in securing the network and governance where ETH holders can vote on protocol upgrades, and major other decisions affecting the Ethereum.

It should also be noted that there is no upper limit on the supply, unlike Bitcoin, but the deflationary nature acts to stabilize the supply and create scarcity in a different manner. However, the initial circulating supply was 119.3 million ETH, but the current supply at the time of writing is 120 million ETH. This may not seem deflationary as such but one must understand how much the ecosystem has grown and therefore there has been a lot of rewards in ETH for mining and more recently, staking rewards for PoS. The issuance was particularly high for the PoW model but is now much lower in PoS. Therefore, despite the growth the supply has remained relatively stable and has begun to become deflationary as a lot of ETH is being burned. It's a balance between utility, scarcity and security.

References

The following references contain more detail from a technical and ecosystem perspective to expand your knowledge:

Ethereum official site with community, FAQs, developer information and architecture:

https://ethereum.org

Ethereum PoS Consensus mechanism, transaction mechanics and checkpoints:

https://ethereum.org/developers/docs/consensus-mechanisms/pos

Weak Subjectivity by Vitalik Buterin:

https://blog.ethereum.org/2014/11/25/proof-stake-learned-love-weak-subjectivity

How checkpoints work in Ethereum:

https://ethereum.org/developers/docs/consensus-mechanisms/pos/weak-subjectivity#ws-checkpoints

ETH issuance information and how the merge impacted ETH supply:

https://ethereum.org/roadmap/merge/issuance

Proto Danksharding:

https://ethereum.org/roadmap/danksharding

Algorand

Brief History

Algorand was founded by computer scientist Silvio Micali, it arose as a solution to the scalability and decentralization challenges faced by existing blockchain platforms.

The project received attention with substantial seed funding in 2018, and an ICO in 2019 which raised over $60 million, introducing the native token, ALGO.

With the official launch of the mainnet in 2019, and later that year, it underwent a large upgrade to Algorand 2.0, introducing features like Smart Contracts and Atomic Transfers.

Since then, it has continued to evolve, addressing scalability concerns and introducing innovations.

What Problem is Algorand Solving?

Much like many blockchains, Algorand is attempting to solve the Trilemma in the following ways:

Decentralization:

Algorand uses a consensus mechanism called Pure Proof of Stake or PPoS (more details on this later in this section). The PPoS algorithm ensures that many participants are involved in the consensus process, enhancing decentralization through a random selection of participants. Although the amount of Algorand that a node owns influences the block proposal via a lottery, the actual amount is not known by other nodes until later in the block proposal and voting phase. This more random selection is what helps achieve decentralization.

Scalability:

Algorand achieves high transaction throughput due to the PPoS algorithm and this allows the network to confirm transactions much more rapidly, allowing it to scale while the user base and transaction volumes also rise. It also offers fast, instant transaction finality because once a block is confirmed, the transactions in that block are instantly considered final. Algorand's 3.16 upgrade reduced the block time to 3.3 seconds with instant finality and recently a new scalability upgrade, Algorand 3.9, enabled a rate of 6000 transactions per second which was demonstrated in testing.

On the topic of finality, Algorand's instant finality is a standout in the blockchain arena because there are currently extremely few chains that can settle transactions instantly in 0ms! Finality is the time it takes for a transaction to become irreversible after a block is written to the chain. Bitcoin for example has a finality time of 60 mins because it has 10-minute blocks, and a transaction is not considered final until 6 confirmations. Algorand requires no confirmations because as soon as a transaction in a block is linked on the chain, that transaction is immediately final and cannot be reversed! As you will find in this chapter, the main reason for this is because a fork in Algorand is not possible. Let's just say theoretically it is, but what if I told you the design is such that the probability is 10 to the power of minus 18?! So practically, there is no chance of a fork. This has also been demonstrated by tests that were run for Algorand's algorithm with a company called Runtime Verification which analyzed and ran all the logic for all input and outputs. More information and demonstration of Algorand's fast transaction speed and finality is included in references in this chapter, as is also the link for Runtime Verification in the References section.

Security:

Through the PPoS consensus mechanism it allows a high degree of security through involving many randomly selected participants in the process. This trait of randomness and the Byzantine Agreement protocol makes the network more resistant to attacks, especially Sybil attacks where an actor creates many accounts to have more weight in decision making. Algorand uses a leader election which uses some facets of PoS and works if at least 2/3 of the actors are honest. This is the Byzantine Agreement protocol, and it can tolerate malicious users, and achieve consensus without a central authority so long as most of the stake is not in malicious hands. Given that the selection of committees is random and secret, the members cannot be bribed, because nobody knows who the committee members are before they have sent their votes. The number of ALGO tokens owned by an account helps to determine the probability of being selected as a block proposer, but the identity of the block proposer is not known until the new block is proposed. This whole mechanism also leads to no possibility of a fork because two blocks cannot be produced at the same time.

Why Pure Proof of Stake?

It's very clear that the PPoS consensus mechanism is at the core of Algorand's solution to the Trilemma. So, let's explore PPoS, how it differs to PoS and what problem it solves.

The following describes the rationale behind Algorand to adopt a PPoS model and why this is such a unique approach in the blockchain sphere.

The whole economy is at the mercy of a small part of the economy

Algorand claims that the PPoS model solves the Trilemma because a critical flaw in almost every blockchain is that "The whole economy is at the mercy of a small part of the economy". This can be explained by the flaw in Proof of Work because only a small part of the economy is owned by the miners. Given that it's the miners that secure the network, then essentially it could be said this is not secure because they own only a small part of the money in that blockchain. For example, if such minority members misbehave, that results in a devaluation of all assets in the economy, including their own assets. However, given that they only form a small part of the economy it's possible they could be compensated while the remaining majority suffer! There should not be a situation where a small subset of the economy controls the whole economy.

With PoS (also known as Bonded Proof of Stake), the nodes need to stake some tokens, essentially a bond which they cannot touch, but if they misbehave some or much of the stake could be slashed. In many blockchains, how much income can someone afford to "hold hostage" on the table? Most would say ideally not very much. Therefore, those with lots of money could put a disproportionate amount of money in the form of many stakes to render control of the blockchain. That is the first flaw claimed by Algorand. The second and larger flaw is the minority is securing the economy for the majority. At the time of writing, about 16% of the circulating supply of ETH in Ethereum is staked.

Delegated PoS is also an issue because the delegates need to remain honest for a long time, but again, they only own a small fraction of the economy.

Algorand's solution

The solution is to tie the security of the whole economy to the honest majority economy. This renders it difficult for the minority to compromise the whole economy. In PPoS, no money is held hostage by slashing stakes or promoting fear by other punishments. Essentially it makes any manipulative behavior by the minority impossible and any manipulation by the majority a very bad idea. This is because in other consensus mechanisms, it's possible for a few nodes to prevent others from transacting or in general a few nodes (or pools) could manipulate the system. In PPoS, only the majority could do this, but doing so would be a stupid idea because it would harm the reputation of the economy if the majority were acting dishonestly!

So, at a very high level, a new block is built as per the following:

- A single ALGO token is selected randomly, and the owner of this token proposes the block.
- A nominal number of tokens, typically 1000 ALGO are selected out of all the tokens in the system. The owners of these tokens then form part of the committee whereby it approves the block proposed by the user.

It's possible that some members may be chosen more than once in which case they will have many votes in the committee to approve the next block.

Why is the committee phase necessary?

Society always has bad actors and although it's difficult to know the percentage of bad actors, it's likely something around 1 or 2 per cent. A more dangerous society would be 10% to 20%. However, no society as we know it would be a majority of bad actors otherwise society would not function well! Society exists in that the people follow the rules at hand.

In the context of Algorand, if we assume that 10% of the tokens are in dishonest hands, that means the chance of a bad actor proposing a block in the initial phase is 10%. As a result, that node may tell other nodes false information about the block leading to a disagreement. The second committee phase removes this issue. If there are 1000 ALGO tokens selected at random and 10% are in malicious hands, then the probability that the majority of the votes belong to bad actors is essentially zero. In the event that a node has not been selected to propose a block or part of the committee, but that node can see a proposed block has 642 votes then that block is the next block to be linked on to the chain.

The big question arises about who selects the committee. The surprising answer is the committee members choose themselves! Of course, this raises an immediate concern being that a member could be a bad actor, but to be a part of the committee the member's ALGO coins must win a cryptographic lottery that is run privately on their machine. Since it's cryptographically fair, the chances of winning cannot be increased.

Therefore, in the case of 1000 tokens out of 10,000,000 then each token has a 1 in 10,000 chance of being selected. Once a user sees a block being proposed that member can take part in the committee to approve the block and gain votes. To take part, the member must run the cryptographic lottery on their machine for each of the tokens owned. There are two possible outcomes which can be either none of the tokens win the lottery or at least one tokens wins. If the former occurs, then the opinion for that member of the proposed block is ignored during the voting phase. If the latter occurs, then there is a proof generated so that others can verify how many votes that member has. This gets broadcast across the network containing the proof of votes and the opinion on the block proposed.

How the committee phase is scalable, secure and decentralized

In terms of scalability, the time it takes to run the cryptographic lottery is a microsecond, no matter how many tokens, so Algorand claims this is scalable even if it's 1000 different users with their own individual votes because this is just 1000 small messages propagated in the system.

In terms of security, members cannot corrupt other members because they don't know who the other members are. This is because the members are selected by a privately run fair lottery and so they only know who they are when the messages are sent through the network revealing the winning tickets and opinions on the block. After this point in time, there is no point trying to corrupt the committee because it's too late because all the opinions and votes have been cast.

In terms of decentralization there is no fixed committee as a different committee is selected every round via the secret lottery.

In addition, Algorand's blockchain cannot fork because there is only one block that has the required threshold of votes and therefore this provides instant finality whereby the transaction is final and cannot be reversed. Algorand claims that the chance of a fork is 10 to the power of minus 18, meaning that a fork may occur once in 10 to the power of 18 seconds, the time since the creation of the universe, the big bang!

The technical details of all this are explained in the next PPoS Detailed Breakdown section.

PPoS Detailed Breakdown

Algorand was the first blockchain to implement PPoS, although there are other variants of it used by Cardano and Tezos. PPoS is a variation of PoS, where the word "pure" means a more direct and somewhat streamlined approach with respect to PoS. This is because it randomizes the selection of participants that create blocks, without knowingly considering the size of their stake. The goal is here to enhance decentralization, therefore not giving power to a few large stakeholders. The randomness also prevents predictability to lower the risk of malicious attacks.

The randomization is done using a **Verifiable Random Function** (VRF). Essentially, this takes a secret key and value to produce a pseudo-random output. Think of this as a lottery which is used to choose a participant to propose blocks and committee members to vote on blocks. This allows a subset of users to be chosen based on their weights, the amount of ALGO they hold. Each user requires a private/public key pair. The VRF then takes an input string and returns an output with two values: a hash and a proof:

- The hash is formed by the user's private key and the input string. It is not possible to decode this without the user's private key.
- The proof allows someone who has the public key (that relates to the private key) of the user to verify that the hash corresponds to the input string for the VRF. The private key is not required because this is just proof verification.

Unlike PoS (and other forms of PoS), PPoS does not have a built-in control mechanism to prevent malicious node activity. This is because it offers lower minimum staking requirements for participation in the network. You only need one ALGO token to become a validator, but in Ethereum, the minimum is 32 ETH. This creates a mechanism where it's not financially viable for bad actors to hijack the network.

Algorand uses the concept of **accounts**, so it is important to understand what an Algorand account is before we delve into how the whole mechanism works.

The two types of accounts are:

- **Offline accounts**: These accounts hold ALGO tokens in the wallet and receive rewards but cannot participate in consensus. However, they can perform any transaction.
- **Online accounts**: To participate in the consensus protocol, as well as holding some ALGO tokens in your wallet the user must register those tokens online. This generates a participation key (which is contained in the node) used for the VRF. In the event this is compromised, the user can still make transactions with the spending key, hence why they are separate.

The consensus mechanism, PPoS for Algorand requires 3 main steps:

- Block Proposal
- Soft Vote
- Certified Vote

The following figure depicts how Algorand's PPoS works:

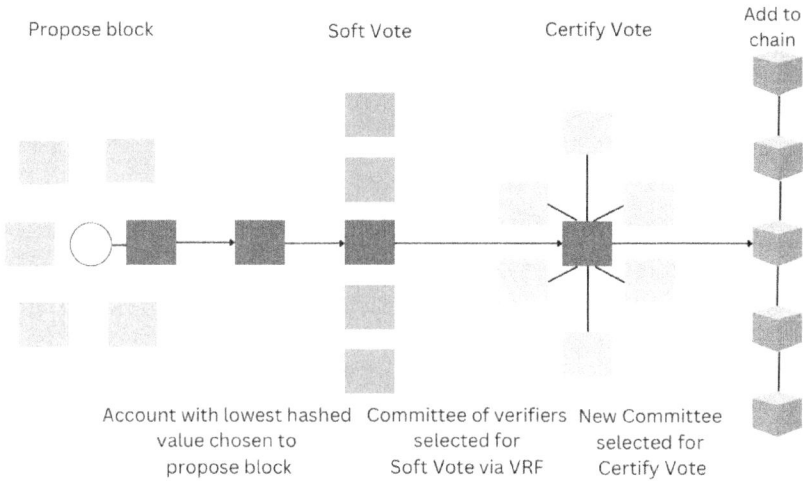

Propose block — Soft Vote — Certify Vote — Add to chain

Account with lowest hashed value chosen to propose block | Committee of verifiers selected for Soft Vote via VRF | New Committee selected for Certify Vote

Block Proposal:

For this step, accounts propose new blocks to the network, which are selected for this round.

- Each node performs the VRF for each account it manages for this round, with a valid participation key.
- A lottery takes place, and this is weighted based on how many ALGO tokens that account has. The more ALGO tokens owned by the account, the higher the probability of being selected. Each ALGO is really like a lottery ticket, so it's possible that an account can be selected more than once in each round.
- Accounts that have won the lottery in this round are extracted.

- Nodes broadcast the blocks proposed by the accounts together with the output of the VRF. This is required to verify that the account has been selected to propose the block.
- A Leader for this round is then selected which is the account with the lowest hashed credential (the certificate generated by the VRF). This is done upon each node receiving a message (containing the proposed block) and checking the length of the hashed credentials. Then based on the length it can decide whether to propagate this message or not. This is called **selective propagation**. This forms part of the Soft Vote phase. There is a point reached where there is only one leader left, and this is the leader for that round.

Soft Vote:

By this phase, each node will have received and sent many block proposals. The objective is through selective propagation (mentioned in the Block Proposal phase), it filters down all the block proposals until there is one left, being the Leader.

- Each node runs the VRF again for each consensus participant account it manages.
- This leads to the extraction of the soft vote committee. Just like in the Block Proposal step, this is a weighted lottery based on the amount of ALGO each account owns.
- Once an account is chosen, that account will then vote for the block proposal with the lowest hashed credential.
- This process continues for a finite period in such a way that there is enough time for votes to be broadcast in the network, but also not to hamper scalability for adding new blocks to the chain.
- Once the voting period has ended, nodes send the votes to the other nodes with the VRF output (this verifies that they are real committee participants for the soft vote).
- Each node validates the VRF as proof of the committee members, then counts the votes. Once a minimum number is reached, based on the size of the committee, this phase is complete.

Note that each time this is rerun, a new committee is selected, and of a different number of participants.

Certified Vote:

- Through VRF again a new committee is formed.
- This committee checks the block proposed from the soft vote phase to verify that block and check for issues such as double spends.
- The committee members conduct a vote to check if the block is valid. The vote is weighted based on the amount of ALGO owned.
- The votes are then sent through the network. The nodes validate the votes by the VRF, until a certain percentage of votes is reached.
- Once the minimum percentage is reached (the quorum), the block is added to the blockchain. This round has now ended, the next round can begin, starting with the Block Proposal phase.

Using this method of block production, two blocks cannot be proposed at the same time, which means this should not result in a fork of the blockchain. Once a block is produced, this means it has achieved consensus and is final, which reduces network latency.

However, there are some potential problems that can occur throughout the 3 phases, such as what if the Certified Vote phase doesn't reach the required number of votes in the finite timeframe? This is where the mechanism enters **Recovery Mode**. This could be due to network issues or malicious behavior. Messages are then sent through the network by Nodes as "Recovery" messages, which indicate whether to continue processing the previous block or propose a new block. If malicious behavior is detected, this may result in the proposal of a new leader.

This recovery mode is used for efficiency for block production because Algorand doesn't make use of slashing to punish bad actors (by reducing their staked balance). This has faced some criticism, but this is the trade-off that has been made.

Algorand Network Architecture

The following depicts the network architecture for the types of nodes and their roles. It illustrates the two types of Nodes being Relay Nodes and Participation Nodes (Non-Relay Nodes):

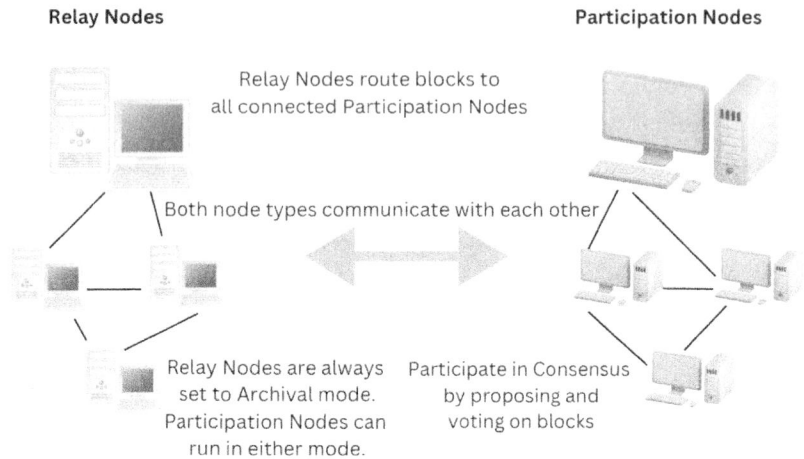

Relay Nodes — Relay Nodes route blocks to all connected Participation Nodes — **Participation Nodes** — Both node types communicate with each other — Relay Nodes are always set to Archival mode. Participation Nodes can run in either mode. — Participate in Consensus by proposing and voting on blocks

Relay Nodes:

Relay nodes do not generally participate in consensus and are always set to Archival Mode. Archival Mode stores the entire ledger, and they can process large quantities of data. If Archival Mode is not enabled only the last 1000 blocks are stored to preserve space.

These nodes always maintain connections to other relay nodes and participation nodes and assist other nodes to make sure they have the same block information, so that the network is always synchronized. They propagate information and check for things like duplicate transactions.

Participation Nodes (Non-Relay):

These nodes participate in consensus and validate transactions, propose and vote on blocks and enhance network security. They don't relay information to other nodes, but rather they rely on relay nodes to receive information and share updates. Participation nodes will not use a relay node unless it is configured when set up. However, one can also configure Relay Nodes to participate in consensus, but this is not recommended as it compromises security. They can be set to use Archival Mode or have it disabled.

Algorand finality and comparison with Solana

Algorand has instant finality and therefore **deterministic finality**. This contrasts with the **probabilistic finality** that other chains have. Probabilistic finality is where there is always a probability that a transaction could be reversed if there is a fork for example. Therefore, as more blocks are added to the chain, the chances of a transaction reversal become lower. Bitcoin has probabilistic finality because there is a chance the chain could fork which could result in a different set of transactions on the forked chain. Probabilistic finality is achieved when a transaction in the block is mined on the longest chain. This is where Bitcoin requires more confirmations where each confirmation lowers the probability of a transaction being reversed. It turns out for Bitcoin thus far; this has not been an issue. However, many chains require extra confirmations and have a chance that a fork could occur, resulting in possible transaction reversal. For more information on forks and orphaned blocks, refer to the Bitcoin chapter.

Let's take an example where you have a blockchain with a block time of 3.3 seconds, but based on the algorithm of the chain, a fork will either succeed or fail within 4 blocks. What this means is that after 4 blocks of 3.3 seconds, about 13 seconds, you can be certain there is a longer chain, and the real chain is the longest chain. If the block time is 3.3 seconds, an additional 4 blocks are required to know if the transaction is final. Given that 13 seconds is your time to finality, from the time you press send, to the time that your transaction is final would be 16.3 seconds.

The issue here is that some get confused with block time and finality, but they are different. The example being Solana which has a block time of 400 milliseconds, but Algorand takes 3.3 seconds to propose a block. Therefore, at first sight many would say Solana is faster (and certainly if measured by tps it is currently much faster). However, if one measures speed by finality, the times to finality are very different. Solana can take up to 32 confirmations (about 12 seconds). However, Algorand, since it cannot fork, has instant finality of 0 seconds.

To demonstrate how this works practically, the following are some links that show sending transactions in Algorand and sending transactions in Solana.

This one is sending a transaction from Coinbase to an Algorand wallet. Look at the time difference between when Coinbase says it is sent versus received. Check at the top of the video:

https://imgur.com/a/AxDpNkv

This link shows sending a transaction from a Coinbase to a Solana wallet. Check the difference in arrival times.

https://imgur.com/a/wsrMhzDD

This is sending a transaction from an Algorand account to another Algorand account. You can see the difference between when it is sent and then received.

https://imgur.com/a/zLG8Jhn

This is sending a transaction from a Solana account to another Solana account.

https://imgur.com/a/ukB00UB

Overall, this is for you as the reader to make your own conclusion. But this is simply to demonstrate that scalability is not just about short block times and high tps. Finality is also important and often considered the superior measure as very high tps can be misleading if the transactions are not final.

PPoS vs PoS

As a recap and summary, the following table shows the differences between PoS and PPoS:

	PoS	PPoS
Overall Approach	More generic and consists of various implementations which vary across different blockchain networks. Validators are chosen to create a new block based on the amount they have staked as collateral. Those who have a higher stake are more likely to act benevolently.	A variation of PoS which is more specific and designed by Algorand. It focuses on simplicity, efficiency, and randomness in the selection of validators. The word "pure" is with the intention of a more streamlined approach.
Validator Selection and Decentralization	Validators with larger stakes have a higher chance of being selected to create new blocks and validate transactions. This can mean those nodes have more influence in consensus.	Validators are selected to create new blocks in a more random fashion. This has the intention to make the network more decentralized.
Security	It relies on the monetary incentive for validators to act honestly due to the financial stake in the network. This can raise concerns about centralization and possible collusion. On the other hand, the higher security budget can be viewed as stronger security as there are penalties and slashing for malicious behavior.	It relies on a protocol (Byzantine Agreement) to achieve consensus through randomly selected participants. The randomness in the selection of validators helps to increase security by preventing predictability and reduces malicious behavior. Possible forks in the network are removed as there is no situation where two blocks can be created at once.
Malicious Activity	Activity by bad actors results in the stake being slashed and penalties.	No slashing or penalties, but a Recovery Mode is used instead where a new Leader may be elected.

New Algorand Updates and Interoperability

Although Algorand is not currently EVM compatible there is a program with a $10 million grant to initiate this. This would allow developers and users to leverage the Ethereum ecosystem and tools on Algorand. However, Algorand also enables interoperability in various ways such as Algorand Standard Assets, Algorand Atomic Transfers and Algorand State Proofs.

Algorand Standard Assets

This allows anyone to create any digital asset on Algorand such as NFTs and stablecoins which can be transferred across different applications that support Algorand.

Algorand Atomic Transfers

This allows users to perform many transactions over various accounts in an atomic operation that is also secure, thus allowing efficient cross-chain swaps of assets.

Algorand State Proofs

This allows users to verify the state of the blockchain including smart contracts, transactions and balances without having to run a full node or trust a middleman. This allows light-weight interactions with blockchains that use state proofs. This was part of Algorand's recent 3.9 upgrade.

In addition, there has been a new upgrade called the **Dynamic Lambda Upgrade** which cuts block times to 2.9 seconds. This is because it now has a dynamic round time that is flexible based on congestion and network demand. Depending on the number of transactions and overall demand, the round time is adjusted appropriately, which on average has lowered block times.

Tokenomics

Total Token Supply

There is a maximum supply of 10,000,000,000 ALGO tokens. The intent with the fixed supply is to relieve inflationary pressures and provide certainty of the number of tokens that will exist. As of September 2022, the circulating supply of ALGO was 6.9 billion. The rest are held by the Algorand foundation in secure wallets consisting of Community and Governance Rewards (1,757 million), Ecosystem support (1,176 million) and Foundation Endowment (363 million).

Initial Launch and Distribution of Tokens

A Dutch Auction was used for the token sale whereby ALGO tokens were sold at lower prices until the entire allocation was sold out or a minimum price was reached. The idea was to ensure a fair initial distribution of tokens driven by the market.

There were vesting periods that took place where there was a gradual release of tokens over time rather than immediate distribution. This was done to promote a fair and long-term commitment for the ecosystem. The Total Distribution is:

- Team, Foundation & Investors - 25.0%
- Public Sale - 30.0%
- Node Running Grant - 25.0%
- Participation Rewards - 17.5%
- End User Grant - 2.5%

Participation Rewards and Staking

Users receive rewards by holding and staking their ALGO tokens and uses a percentage-based annual reward, which helps secure the network. Token holders can participate in consensus by staking their tokens.

Governance

This is a decentralized initiative that allows holders to vote on decisions regarding the future of Algorand. Holders that commit for a three-month period enable them to vote on new proposals by the Foundation. This results in rewards for the owners. There are three-month cycles which consist of a sign up, voting and rewards phase. In periods during 2023, rewards were in the order of 5.6% to 9.77%. Governance is completely self-custodial. No minimum amount of ALGO is required to stake for Governance and no node is required to be run.

Fee burn

Transaction fees are paid in ALGO but there is also a fee burn mechanism, where a portion of the transaction fees are burned, which helps to reduce the overall supply. This creates a deflationary nature for the token which should have positive impacts on the price.

References

The following references contain more detail from a technical and ecosystem perspective to expand your knowledge:

Information about tokenomics and latest news:

https://www.algorand.foundation/

Summary of how Algorand solves the Trilemma, the Mission and Team:

https://algorandtechnologies.com/technology/solving-the-blockchain-trilemma

Governance and Staking Rewards:

https://algonaut.space/algorand-staking/

Algorand's link to Runtime Verification to prove it will never fork:

https://medium.com/algorand/formal-verification-of-the-algorand-protocol-bbde5a52b830

Algorand General FAQ:

https://www.algorand.foundation/general-faq#governance-faq-header

Solana

Brief History

In 2017 the founder and CEO, Anatoly Yakovenko, released a whitepaper describing a new consensus mechanism called Proof of History (PoH) in combination with Proof of Stake, which allows very high scalability and is essentially the first blockchain to achieve such a high number of transactions per second (tps) on its mainnet.

PoH is an approach of time keeping between computers that don't naturally trust each other and Anatoly realized that a reliable clock could make the synchronization of nodes in a network much easier, leading to a more efficient blockchain.

Anatoly, with the help of Greg Fitzgerald, programmed the codebase in a language called Rust to increase performance and safety. In 2018, Fitzgerald produced a prototype of Anatoly's whitepaper showcasing 10,000 tps and Solana officially launched in March 2020.

It was designed with smart contracts and dApps in mind which require high performance. This has brought up many challenges, resulting in outages, as Solana pushes the boundaries, but Solana is still evolving as a highly scalable solution for the blockchain world.

What Problem is Solana Trying to Solve?

Many blockchains such as Ethereum or Bitcoin don't have a reliable clock which makes it more difficult for nodes to synchronize. As a result, they struggled to scale, achieving only 15 tps and Anatoly realized that a reliable clock was critical to achieve high scalability.

A problem that other blockchains have is that they must agree on time and nodes on the network must chat back and forth until they agree on a certain time which they must do before submitting a block, but this chatter can take lots of time.

Solana resolves this by having nodes timestamp their blocks using a cryptographic proof, so they don't have to wait for other nodes to agree on the time. The agreement on the organization of data in blocks can be made after the fact, meaning it's not necessary to wait for other validators to check this.

In terms of Solana's consensus mechanism, it uses PoH in addition to PoS to leverage scalability.

Proof of History

Proof of History (PoH) is a cryptographic technique that establishes the order and timestamps of transactions on the Solana blockchain, allowing validators to verify the sequence of transactions. Validators can independently verify the order of events without the need to communicate with each other, which allows the network to process many transactions per second relative to other blockchains.

Proof of Stake

Solana also incorporates Proof of Stake (PoS) as well as PoH where, of course, PoS is widely adopted in other blockchains due to its energy efficiency.

In PoS validators are chosen based on the number of SOL tokens they wish to stake as collateral, and this maintains the security and consensus of the network by validating transactions and producing new blocks. Validators are incentivized to act honestly as they are rewarded with transaction fees and issued new SOL tokens. Any malicious behavior results in those validators losing their staked tokens.

Also, SOL token holders can delegate their tokens to validators, which means they can receive rewards without actively participating in the process of validation, which helps more active engagement in securing the network.

Due to this approach of using PoH in combination with PoS, Solana can process over 3000 to 5000 transactions per second currently and can theoretically scale up to 710,000 tps. In benchmark testing it has already shown speeds of about 50,000 tps. Solana has a very innovative approach that allows for horizontal scaling, so as the network expands, it can handle higher transaction loads with no compromise to performance. This has positioned Solana as a very attractive platform, where it can support a wide range of use cases.

Solana's Consensus Mechanism

This section describes the operation of Solana's consensus where PoS and PoH are used. Given that PoS has been largely described in this book, this focuses more on the details of PoH.

Why Proof of History?

To understand what PoH is, we first need to grasp the concept of time and how it is referenced. Time is a concept used throughout civilization. At one point, time was calculated by how high the sun was in the sky, where each region had its own version of time. This approach worked well because different cities or towns didn't communicate with each other.

Once transportation arrived, communication between regions got faster so time was more critical as people needed to know what time they would arrive in another city. Time zones were then created to standardize between different regions.

With the advent of computers communication speeds became critical and therefore so did time zones. Electronic devices would need to synchronize with a central clock on the internet to make sure their internal clocks were accurate. This is all very well when devices rely on centralized services, but what happens in a distributed computer environment where there is no central clock, like blockchains? Many like Bitcoin, rely on a median timestamp and that's how it manages transactions in the order they were received. This works but is a much slower approach as lots of chatter is required to agree on the correct timestamps and order transactions and blocks.

Solana addresses this problem by implementing Proof of History, where timestamps for all events are built into the ledger. This is achieved by a **verifiable delay function (VDF)**, which each producer of a block must run.

Data is inserted in a sequence where the hash of the data is appended to the previously generated states. The state and input data are used and it's impossible to generate other versions of this. This sets up an upper bound on time and because Proof of History can reference previous hashes, there is also a lower bound of time. Essentially a VDF is a function that is run that takes an input and generates an output. It's not possible to predict this output without running the function, and this can all be chained together where the output of the last function supplies the input to the next. The chaining is achieved with a cryptographic hash function, and this provides verifiable moments in time.

Therefore, rather than using a human style clock, a different clock is used based on the time it takes to run a function (specifically a SHA-256 hash function) several times over. This time is measured in something called **"ticks"** which is many hash iterations as a fraction of a second. For example, 100,000 iterations may represent one second. This can then show when in the past or future a transaction occurred in relation to a state machine. The ticks are essentially a way to abstract the time in terms of computers based on the frequency of the processor's clock where a 1GHz processor has a clock cycle that lasts 1 nanosecond where 1 tick is one nanosecond. But different systems have different clock speeds so using ticks allows us to measure the speed in operations relative to the system's clock. Therefore, the speed of the SHA-256 hashing function run by the VDF may be slower or faster on different machines than the average achieved by machines across the network, but from the view of the network the same number of ticks has passed.

The VDF ensures that there is a verifiable and secure method to keep time in the network without a centralized clock, which is vital for ordering transactions.

The sequence of steps a VDF takes are the following:

- It receives some input data, specifically on the first run, a seed value, which can be any number or a string of characters.
- It runs a sequence of operations where this sequence takes a predictable amount of time to calculate, where part of the sequence is solving a problem for example.
- This then outputs a hash value that is unique to the input.

- This output hash is now the input to the next VDF.
- There is a count recorded as well as the output to create a record that can be publicly verified. This proves that a certain event, for example, a transaction, occurred at a certain point in time relative to other events.

The VDF is delay-hard meaning that it is designed to take time to compute as it's like solving a mathematical problem with certain inputs and this requires a predictable amount of time which cannot be sped up by running more processors in parallel. This allows Solana to process transactions very quickly and securely.

The following illustrates the VDF with the context of input data and transactions. A validator includes the PoH sequence values, akin to a timestamp (calculated from the VDF), and with the transactions in the proposed block:

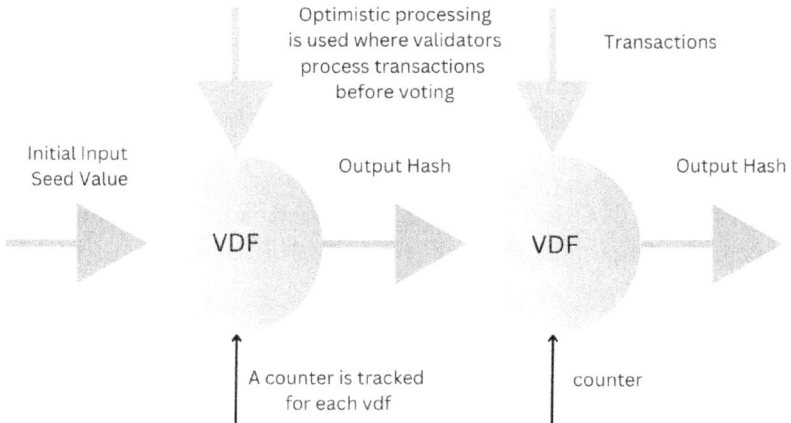

The **Seed** is a random value used as input where the VDF repeatedly applies a specific function to this initial value. From then on it takes the previous hash that was output, as its next input and runs the VDF on that.

160

Essentially the output hash represents a specific point in the sequence, analogous to a timestamp in the human world, acting like a reference point for events, where each hash builds upon the previous one to maintain the order.

Now that PoH has been described, the next section shows how this is integrated and used in the consensus mechanism with Proof of Stake and why it's crucial in achieving scalability.

The operation of Proof of History and Proof of Stake

Whereas Proof of Stake can maintain consensus if most nodes are honest, there is no guarantee this can occur with high throughput. Proof of History allows this to happen at a much faster rate while still maintaining security.

The first thing that must be considered is that there only needs to be one node that submits a proposed block, otherwise many other nodes would submit blocks at the same time. This would make things complicated because there would then need to be many branches (or forks) of the blockchain to choose based on fork choice algorithms, which is not desirable. This one node is called the **Leader** and just like in Ethereum there is a block proposer that can be chosen by a validator committee, in Solana the Leader gets chosen.

The leader is selected based on a random number generator (specifically a Verifiable Random Function or VRF) and its stake weight. This leader is assigned a slot in an epoch (much like in Ethereum and other PoS chains). In Solana however, there are 432,000 slots in an epoch where each slot is about 400 milliseconds and therefore an epoch is about 2 to 3 days in duration. The leader schedule is determined two epochs before the current epoch, which gives a lot of time for all validators to know the leader schedule in advance.

In Solana, there is an overlap of transmission of a block and processing transactions which contributes to its high scalability. This is because while the leader is running the VRF it is essentially encoding the passage of time, akin to timestamping and at the same time, verifying the transactions. As the validator streams the transactions it is also computing the PoH sequence values with it, so since the timestamping of events is being carried out during this phase, other validators don't need to be consulted later to validate this. When the slot finishes and the output hash has been generated, this provides proof that the operations have been run and encoding of time has been completed. The next leader then takes the output hash as its input and provides verifiable proof that it has started where the previous leader finished. It couldn't have done this before because the operations in the VRF took time to run. So, this provides a Proof of History for that slot proving that the block was generated in that slot, at that time, and this can be verified by other validators together with a signature that the leader output for that slot. This confirms that the block was produced at that time by that leader, making it very difficult for a competing leader to output a block in that same slot. There is an example later in this chapter which highlights why other rogue, competing or malicious leaders cannot produce competing blocks for a slot very easily.

Since there are 432,000 slots per epoch, of course, there would not be enough unique leaders practically for each slot, so a given leader can emit blocks for different slots within the same epoch. However, given that the leader schedule is known in advance, all leaders are known by the validators two epochs ahead and so blocks must be generated in the order given by the schedule.

For example, if there are 6 leaders the schedule, and therefore block generation order, may look like this:

L1, L2, L6, L4, L1, L3, L5, L2, L5, L6, L4, ...

At the end of an epoch, there is a global state that is output, and this is then used as part of a random number generator (via a VRF), to select the next set of leaders (in two epochs time). Since this global state is the combination of a set of values by many validators, there is no way for a particular validator to control or influence any particular outcome because these values are not predictable by any individual node.

Now that leaders have submitted their blocks a vote occurs as per the usual PoS mechanism.

- Validators vote on the proposed blocks submitted by the leaders.
- Votes are stake-weighted, meaning validators with more collateral have more influence on the outcome.

162

- The network reaches consensus when a supermajority of validators agrees on a block.

Solana vs Ethereum and other PoS blockchains

The important thing to understand is that although Ethereum and other PoS blockchains use a similar mechanism of a block proposer or leader to submit blocks and a way to schedule them two epochs in advance, Solana also submits the timestamp for all events at the same time, thus requiring no extra validation. The timestamping provided by PoH is used to sequence transactions before they are even finalized in a block. In other PoS chains, it relies on the validators to attest to them and uses a fork choice rule to finalize the order of blocks and transactions. This creates extra chatter and takes longer.

To gain more understanding, let's explore what a **fork choice rule** is and why the probability of different branches of a chain (or forks) is less in Solana. A fork choice rule refers to the method of how nodes decide which blockchain branch is the true version of the blockchain, known as the canonical chain. A fork choice arises when multiple valid blocks are submitted for the same slot, whereby a fork occurs, thus creating multiple branches.

This rule helps nodes to choose between these different branches. In Ethereum 2.0 for example, this rule is part of its consensus and makes sure that nodes all agree on the same history for the blockchain. This also helps to resolve forks even where there are attempts to disrupt the blockchain and helps nodes to converge on the same chain.

Since Solana creates a historical record of events, this establishes a chronological order of transactions, which is woven into the ledger, and therefore, all nodes have a consistent view of the order of transactions, which is vital for preventing forks. Once a transaction is recorded with a timestamp via the VDF, it is already ordered and cannot be altered and therefore the network rarely needs to employ fork choice rules at a later point. In the rare event that two competing blocks are submitted for the same slot, the voting process and fork choice rules in Solana will handle this.

Another main difference is in the handling of collusion. Solana does not use a PBS (Proposer Builder Separation) mechanism like Ethereum where a validator that builds a block cannot also propose that same block. This design approach in Ethereum is to help prevent collusion amongst other reasons, but Solana's collusion prevention is achieved with the PoH encoding of time as mentioned earlier. Some argue that Ethereum has better prevention of collusion with its PBS approach, but overall, Solana has prioritized speed with a balance of also preventing collusion. Different blockchains make different design choices based on which facets of the Trilemma they want to optimize. This collusion risk is not unique to Solana and there is risk with all chains.

The summary in terms of **collusion risk from a PBS perspective** is this:

Ethereum 2.0:

- PBS enhances decentralization and censorship resistance.
- Validators specialize in either proposing or building blocks.
- Collusion risk still exists.

Solana:

- There is no explicit proposer builder separation (PBS).
- Validators handle both roles of a proposer of blocks and a builder of blocks, which also aids throughput.
- Solana's approach with PoH and using a random number generator to select leaders make it difficult for a validator to influence others because these values are not predictable by an individual validator.
- Some collusion risk exists but is not unique to Solana.

This following table summarizes the difference between Solana and Ethereum in terms of consensus, timing and scalability:

	Solana	Ethereum
Slots per epoch	432,000	32
Timestamps for events	Passage of time encoded via a VDF akin to a timestamp	Not using a VDF, conventional timestamp is added for each block
Ordering of transactions	Mainly ordered as per the VDF which requires less chatter in the voting and fork choice phases	Agreed and ordered mainly during the attestation (voting) and fork choice phases
Known leader or block proposer schedule	2 epochs in advance (2-3 days)	2 epochs in advance (12.8 minutes)
Scalability approach	Streams transactions in batches and computes PoH sequence values at the same time	Sharding and other layer 2s such as rollups
Current number of transactions per second	3000 - 5000	15 - 30

Example of PoH addressing malicious behavior

Let's say we have 4 leaders L1, L2, L3 and L4 where L1 is the first and L4 is the last.

So, the schedule is:

L1, L2, L3, L4

L1 has generated its block then L2 can produce its block. If L3 wants to cheat the system and produce a block while in L2's slot, let's see what happens.

This means L3 must link to L1's block, but this is contrary to the leader schedule. Also, if L3 produces a block that has the same PoH as L2 then other validators

165

would know L3 is cheating the system because it emitted its block in L2's slot. The only way around this is that L3 needs to make it look as if L2 never produced a block. That would look like this:

L1, no block, L3, L4

So, if L2 was missing, then L3 would have to use all L2's slot producing a PoH sequence and proving that it waited the full time of L2's slot before starting its own slot. L3's block would be accepted as valid because this is in the correct slot as per the schedule.

So L3 must demonstrate that it waited for L2's slot before starting its block by calculating many PoH hashes for that slot. At the same time however, L2 is generating its block that branches from L1, and therefore L1 produces a valid block with a full PoH. Then L2 begins streaming its block, so from the network's perspective, L2 is producing a block properly branched from L1 with a valid PoH.

One of the following can now occur:

- If L3 cannot compute PoH faster than L2, then L2 will finish its block around the same time that L3 produces its block branched from L1. However, L3's block was rejected by the network because it has already seen L2's block.
- If L3 computes PoH faster than L2, it can start emitting its block before L2 has sent its block. In this scenario, L3 has a higher chance of winning than the scenario above but it's still not likely unless L3 is significantly faster than L2. It would need to be so much faster to the point where it sends its block before a large portion of L2's block is viewed by the network.

Some final points on this are:

- Most validators would have CPUs running at a speed quite close to each other whereby the time in computing hashes, and therefore a PoH, wouldn't stray very much. So L3's speed in relation to L2 would have to be much faster to compete for a block in L2's slot, effectively censoring L2.

- In the highly likely situation that L3 loses in its attempt to compete for L2's slot, this means L3 would be slashed as it has invalidated the rules. This is because if it loses and now attempts to submit a different block for its slot (branched off L2's slot) this means there are now two different blocks for L3's slot: an L1, L3 block and an L2, L3 block. This is not allowed and given the high probability of failure this means L3 is deemed to fail, thus making it a foolish attempt.

Solana Network Architecture

The following illustrates the Solana Architecture where a transaction occurs, and Leaders receive the transaction forwarded from an RPC server.

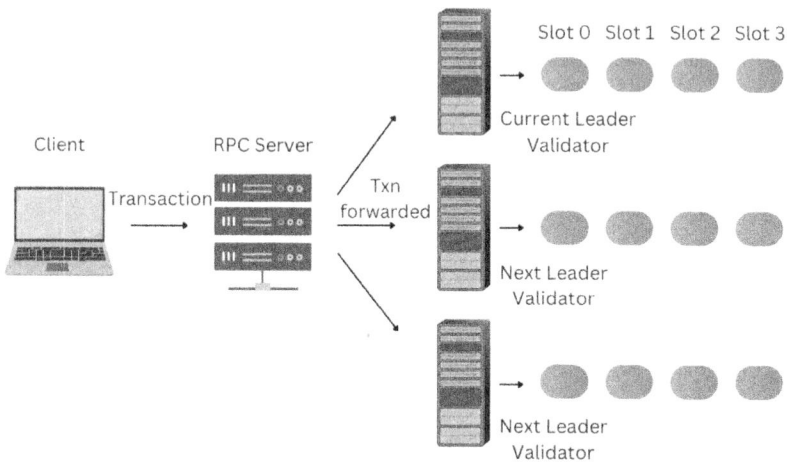

The steps that occur are:

- A user signs the transaction in their wallet, and it then gets sent to a Solana RPC server (these can be run by any validator).
- Once the transaction is received by the RPC server, the leader schedule is checked.

- It then forwards the transaction to the current leader and the next two leaders. The reason for forwarding to the next two leaders is because this helps with redundancy whereby if the current leader is unable to process the transaction due to technical issues, then the next leader can take over. Also, if nodes come and go offline, as can be the case in an unpredictable decentralized network, then this mechanism can deal with this and keep the network stable.

Note that in this example the Leaders have been assigned consecutive slots. The Leader Schedule may assign Leaders some consecutive slots or not depending on the way the schedule is set up. For this example, consecutive slots have been shown for simplicity. However, it's typical that consecutive slots in groups of four can be scheduled for a given Leader which can help performance. This is because transactions can be processed with lower latency, as the Leader doesn't need to pass the processing to the next Leader immediately.

Upcoming Features

This section describes some of the upcoming features as part of the Solana roadmap with the vision to make it more decentralized, scalable and flexible.

Token Extensions

Token extensions help to enhance the functionality of tokens on Solana. This includes:

Custom Transfer Logic: Developers can program customized logic controlling how tokens are transferred.

Confidential Transfers: Allows for privacy in the transfer of tokens, which can hide the number of tokens transferred and allow optional auditing at the same time.

Extended Metadata: Tokens can contain extra metadata to provide richer interactions and more context for transactions themselves.

168

Platform Interoperability

Solana is increasing interoperability with other blockchain platforms such as **Chainlink** where decentralized oracles interact with Solana's smart contracts to provide real-world data.

The **Solana Bridge** (also called AllBridge), built on the IBC protocol, allows for asset transfers and provides other services such as borrowing and lending across different blockchains allowing for cross-chain Interoperability. This is a broader approach to being interoperable with many blockchains via IBC.

More specifically, Solana is also working to interoperate with platforms such as Ethereum and Polygon. The Wormhole Bridge was developed not by Solana as such but by Certus One in partnership with the Solana Foundation. This allows Solana to interoperate with EVM chains and is thus a more dedicated bridge for those chains. Although this is a significant step, which facilitates the transfer of assets between Solana and Ethereum, the roadmap includes improving existing bridges like Wormhole but also developing new protocols that could further streamline and secure cross-chain interactions to other non-EVM chains. The Solana Bridge, AllBridge, is an example of this on a broader level. Also, advancements in zero-knowledge proofs are being explored which allows more efficient and private approaches to connect different blockchains. There are also efforts to standardize cross-chain communication protocols to make a smoother approach for developers to build applications that can operate on many different chains in a seamless manner.

The Solana team is also continuing to make their platform more accessible to Ethereum developers by improving EVM compatibility and creating tools that make it easier to port applications from Ethereum to Solana.

There are also other updates such as a decentralized exchange called **Serum** being built that provides benefits in terms of scalability.

Overall, it's clear that Solana is continuously innovating and pushing the boundaries, which carries some risk in introducing bugs or vulnerabilities but thus far it has been very successful in becoming a major player in the blockchain space, certainly from a scalability perspective.

Tokenomics

Initial launch and token distribution

Solana launched with an initial supply of 500 million tokens. Its maximum supply is uncapped with a disinflationary emission rate, where the supply of SOL tokens is sought to reach about 700 million by 2030. The overall inflation rate is a combination of the initial inflation (8%), the disinflation rate (-15%) and the long-term inflation rate (1.5%). What this means is that the initial inflation rate is 8% per year, decreasing by 15% each year, and reaching a fixed inflation rate long-term of 1.5% per year.

A large portion of the inflation is paid to those with staked SOL tokens and essentially, it's based on the amount of SOL staked divided by the total amount of SOL staked in the network, hence the percentage of SOL staked. Stakers can be those who delegate their stake to a validator or a validator itself.

The distribution of Solana tokens is as below:

Private sale: 35%

Public sale: 15%

Team and Advisors: 10%

Solana Foundation: 20%

Ecosystem: 20%

SOL token utility

SOL is a utility token to pay for transaction fees on the Solana network and is also used by validators who secure the network, by staking a certain amount of SOL tokens. Staking encourages validators to behave honestly as it acts as collateral and validators earn additional SOL tokens for partaking in consensus. Also, holders of the SOL token can participate in the governance of the Solana network, allowing token holders to vote on changes, and improvements to the protocol. The more SOL tokens held by each participant, the higher the governance power they have.

When transactions occur, 50% of the gas fee is burned which means that part of the fee is removed from circulation permanently. This helps to reduce the overall supply and boost the value of the SOL token. The remaining 50% is distributed to the validator that processed the transaction. This maintains a balance between burning of the SOL token and rewarding validators.

References

The following links provide more detail on the Solana ecosystem:

Information about the ecosystem on the official site such as validator setup, community events, latest news and Solana documentation:

https://solana.com/

Solana's inflation schedule:

https://solana.com/docs/economics/inflation/inflation_schedule

Transaction fee burning:

https://solana.com/docs/intro/transaction_fees

Proof of History (PoH) innovation and analogies:

https://solana.com/news/proof-of-history

Information on statistics such as tps and staking pools:

https://solanacompass.com/

Solana whitepaper:

https://solana.com/solana-whitepaper.pdf

The Solana Bridge (AllBridge):

https://solana.com/ecosystem/allbridge

Pulsechain

Brief History

PulseChain created by Richard Heart, the founder of HEX cryptocurrency, launched in May 2023, where it is the first full-state hard fork of the Ethereum blockchain. It has 10 second blocks making it about 17% faster than Ethereum and seeks to reduce the pressure and load on the Ethereum network whereby those who move across to Pulsechain reduce the congestion on Ethereum. Given that PulseChain is essentially a copy of Ethereum, that also means it's a PoS network, thus making it more energy efficient than PoW chains.

Another key to this is being a full-state fork meant this wasn't a typical hard fork because it also copied the full state of the Ethereum blockchain meaning all ERC 20 tokens and smart contracts were copied! Upon launch, everyone received a copy of the ERC 20 tokens on Pulsechain which made it the largest airdrop in history.

Prior to the launch there was a sacrifice phase which allowed participants to sacrifice their existing cryptocurrencies (such as ETH, HEX, and other ERC20 tokens) in exchange for PulseChain's native token, known as PLS. This was a sacrifice for free speech. There were no expectations of profit as there was no guarantee that anyone who sacrificed their cryptocurrency would receive any Pulsechain tokens in return. In addition, anyone who did receive tokens would receive them at a value of zero. Market discovery would then set the price after launch.

A second sacrifice phase also occurred in exchange for Pulsechain's native DEX token called PulseX where participants received PLSX tokens. Each phase lasted for a certain time after which no more contributions could be made. Those who sacrificed their tokens received PLS tokens (for the Pulsechain Sacrifice) and PLSX tokens (for the PulseX sacrifice) in return, based on how much they sacrificed, where the more that was sacrificed, the more respective tokens they received. Overall, the sacrifice phases played a key role in bootstrapping the PulseChain network.

Pulsechain's full state hard fork vs typical hard forks

Unlike typical hard forks, PulseChain took a different approach by replicating the entire state of the Ethereum blockchain meaning that it copied the ERC-20 tokens and smart contracts and the entire history of transactions and balances. This could be thought of as a parallel universe where the state of Ethereum was copied at a certain point in time.

However, most normal hard forks operate differently because instead of replicating the entire state, they usually fork from a certain block and the new chain begins from that chosen block. An example of this was Ethereum Classic which forked from Ethereum where in that case, only the state from that specific block is copied going forward.

What Problem is Pulsechain Trying to Solve?

One of the main issues of contention was the high gas fees on Ethereum. This was also causing a lot of pain for HEX holders because the cost of using HEX on Ethereum was very high due to the high fees. This was a major issue that instigated the move to fork Ethereum to Pulsechain. The major details of HEX and how it works are outside the scope of this book, but to get more context lets understand at a high level what HEX is and why it was pivotal in the shift to Pulsechain.

Description of HEX

HEX is a cryptocurrency that resides as a smart contract built on Ethereum blockchain and now more recently on Pulsechain (where all smart contracts were copied). This is a very unique product which attracted a lot of attention on launch in 2019.

In simple terms HEX is generally viewed as a CD (Certificate of Deposit) on the blockchain. A CD in legacy finance is where people lock up their money for a certain period and the longer the lockup period the higher the interest they receive. Some argue HEX is not strictly a CD because a CD in the legacy financial world is more stable in that locking up fiat dollars guarantees that a 5% return for that lockup period cannot change in dollar terms. However, the HEX payout at the end of the lockup period is in HEX, not in dollars, and HEX is subject to volatility in price. On the other hand, some would say that this is a different product and doesn't need to be a legacy style finance product because this is blockchain world, it's meant to be different! Since the payout is in HEX, if one thinks in HEX terms then it's a very stable and reliable payout. Comparing it to a CD is more to help people to relate and understand the product rather than it trying to be a CD per se. HEX took many concepts from a CD because locking up larger amounts of HEX and for longer pays more yield.

The product attracted a lot of attention because it's an immutable smart contract with no upgrades unlike a project that contains a roadmap promising new features that may or may not get delivered or introduce bugs as a result. HEX is a finished product, and it was launched as complete with no extra updates planned, which is somewhat unusual in the blockchain space. This is seen as a strength in terms of making it robust and more secure due to less risk of introducing new bugs. One huge security feature unlike many cryptocurrencies is that during the lockup period the HEX is burned meaning that even if the smart contract was hacked, the hacker cannot get the HEX! At the end of the lockup period all the HEX principle plus yield is minted. A major innovation in HEX is the idea that locking up the tokens prevents holders from selling early and therefore delaying gratification, as long-term investing is a very good practice in general. This contrasts with many projects in the blockchain space.

The problems on Ethereum began when the gas fees soared because the HEX smart contract calls a function to unlock the HEX at the end of the lockup period to pay the yield. This function costs a lot of gas, especially for longer lockup periods. This made using the product very painful, so as a result, the founder proposed a cheaper, faster and more decentralized blockchain called Pulsechain. This would allow users of HEX to lock up for long periods for much cheaper fees and using a block time of 10 seconds rather than Ethereum's 13 second blocks would give a scalability increase too. However, this was just the beginning as there was a lot more to Pulsechain than just a new chain dedicated to HEX. It would copy all smart contracts and ERC 20s allowing users to speculate and set up liquidity pools for those copies (known as PRC 20s). It also brought some new game theory with it, quite like no other blockchain. This is all discussed in the next section called Pulsechain Game Theory.

Scalability

Pulsechain set out to improve transactions processed per second by implementing 10 second blocks yielding a 17% increase with respect to Ethereum. The long-term scalability roadmap is unclear, but it has been proposed that if Pulsechain eventually suffers from the same bottlenecks that Ethereum has then another parallel blockchain could be built! This could be another fork of the existing Pulsechain using a horizontal scaling approach. This is all just speculation as it's a long way until Pulsechain becomes so congested like Ethereum, if at all, depending on the level of adoption.

Improving Game Theory and Tokenomics

This is described in detail in the next section, but the summary is that Pulsechain aimed to solve many of the flaws in tokenomics that other blockchains have.

Inflation:

One flaw that many blockchains have in their tokenomics is that many are inflationary because they have a pre-sale where the team, developers and VCs are allocated tokens where a percentage are locked initially then gradually unlocked over a period of years. The problem is the initial price of the token does not cater for all the new tokens becoming unlocked over the next few years. Pulsechain's PLS and PLSX tokens were all allocated on launch to everyone who sacrificed and were set at a finite supply which always decreases, thus making it **deflationary**. There were no more tokens to be issued or unlocked after a certain period, meaning no more inflation or dilution of holders' wallets.

Burning of tokens:

Many blockchains use a burning mechanism to control the supply of tokens. However, this may help the price in the long-term, but this does not have an immediate effect on price because simply burning tokens reduces the supply but doesn't increase the demand. A higher price relies on low supply and high demand, but burning only lowers the supply.

Pulsechain's native DEX called PulseX uses a **buy and burn** mechanism. The idea is to have a greater effect on the price of PLSX because this now reduces the supply and increases the demand. This works whereby each transaction that occurs on the PulseX DEX buys up a portion of PLSX and then burns it. If one compares this to Uniswap (which is not deflationary at all, but rather inflationary), this appears to be an improvement given the growth of the UNI token which compared to other cryptocurrencies has not had huge price appreciation. This is a surprise given Uniswap's adoption. The largest DEX by daily volume has not been able to reflect this in the price of its native token. PulseX aims to solve this by making sure that increased adoption is reflected by the price as the more transactions that occur the more PLSX is bought and burned. Therefore, the increased adoption increases the price of PLSX, so essentially if the PulseX DEX performs well and gets more adoption, the price of PLSX reflects this performance.

Pulsechain Game Theory

The strongest component in Pulsechain lays in its game theory. As already mentioned, both the foundation layer, Pulsechain itself, and the native DEX, PulseX boast some impressive game theory.

Pulsechain

The native token PLS has a maximum supply of 136 trillion tokens. This uses a deflationary model where each transaction burns the base fee, just like Ethereum. However, in addition, Pulsechain burns an extra 25% for each transaction, meaning that Pulsechain has an extra 25% fee burn in addition to EIP-1559. In more simplistic terms, this means a portion of the tip fee is burned (unlike Ethereum where none of the tip fee is burned). Since the supply can never exceed 136 trillion, the supply gradually reduces making it deflationary.

Pulsechain also requires validators to stake 32,000,000 PLS as a pre-requisite (similar in concept to Ethereum where 32 ETH is required). This helps to take a large portion of PLS off the market because PLS that is staked is not part of the circulating supply. Currently, there are 50,000 validators running on Pulsechain, so this amounts to approximately 1.59 trillion PLS staked, which is more than 1% of the maximum supply! That is a lot of PLS removed from the market.

In summary, the extra 25% burn for each transaction and high number of validators reduces the supply and takes a portion of the supply off the market respectively, which is good for price providing there is high demand.

PulseX

The native token PLSX has a maximum supply of 142 trillion tokens. This also uses a deflationary mechanism whereby each transaction on the PulseX DEX buys up and burns a portion of PLSX. The addition of buying as well as burning makes the game theory for PLSX quite unique, and for that reason, it's more deflationary than PLS.

The way it works is when a user does a swap on PulseX a 0.29% fee is applied. Think of this as like trading fees on centralized exchanges. Out of this fee, 21% is used to buy PLSX and then burn it, and the remainder goes to the liquidity providers. So, for every transaction, a specific amount of PLSX is bought from the market and removed from the circulating supply. This creates buy pressure and reduces the supply, which helps to increase the value of PLSX overall.

The following illustrates this for a given transaction on the PulseX DEX:

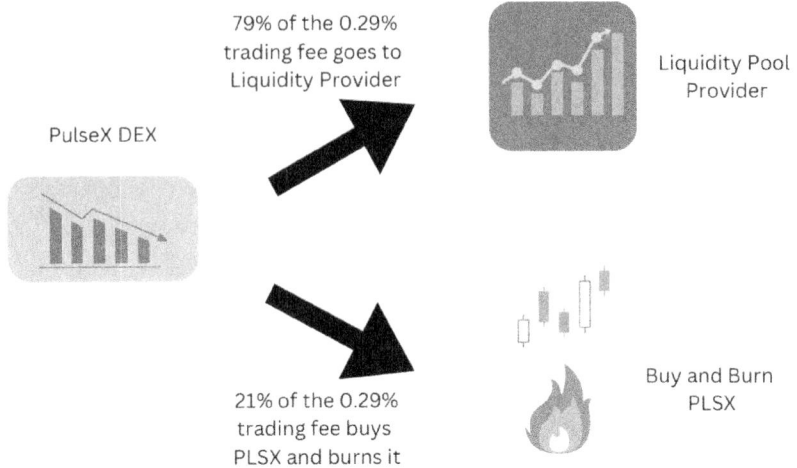

PulseX DEX

79% of the 0.29% trading fee goes to Liquidity Provider

Liquidity Pool Provider

21% of the 0.29% trading fee buys PLSX and burns it

Buy and Burn PLSX

If we also consider that for a swap for on PulseX, that a percentage of PLSX is burned in proportion to the volume that is swapped. This is what makes PLSX even more deflationary again because unlike PLS, where a portion of PLS is burned per gas fee for a transaction, PLSX is burned in relation to the whole volume traded for a transaction! So, for a $10,000 swap, a 0.29% fee is applied, where 21% of that 0.29% buys up and burns PLSX. If the PLSX price is $0.0001, that's equivalent to 100,000,000 PLSX in volume traded, where about 60,000 PLSX would be bought up then burned, and the higher the volume the more burned. Note this is a very simple example. PLSX is bought up and burned for any transaction of PulseX. PLSX doesn't have to be directly part of the swap. For example, if swapping HEX to HDRN, PLSX is still bought up and burned based on the volume of this swap.

As a result, at the time of writing almost one trillion PLSX has been burned out of the total 142 trillion supply, in about one year! In summary, with increased adoption, the PLSX price will reflect this adoption accordingly which helps provide a great incentive mechanism to use the DEX. In addition to this, other DEXs such as PHUX and 9-inch have since been built on Pulsechain by a very flourishing, strong community, allowing more options and choice based on fees for example.

There is more information on the PulseX DEX and providing liquidity in the References section.

Incentive Token

The Incentive Token, called INC is used to reward those who participate in Pulsechain yield farms and Liquidity Pools. Tokens that are staked in farms earn yield directly in INC. Also, a Liquidity Provider earns yield in both tokens that are added to a liquidity pool, but those tokens can then be staked in farms to earn INC. So essentially the LPs earn INC indirectly.

INC is an inflationary token, but the inflation reduces over time, making it **disinflationary**. The inflation rate drops from 50% in the third year from launch to 33% in year 4, to 25% in year 5, 20% in year 6 all the way to 11% in year 10.

The interesting aspect is that this is another major token (in addition to PLS, PLSX and HEX) in the Pulsechain ecosystem that can have price appreciation. Note that these are the only four tokens in the ecosystem that were all created by the founder and team, which is also why INC has gained a lot of attention. By staking any tokens in Pulsechain (not just these four) in farms helps to lock up those tokens, removing them from the circulating supply, thus aiding those tokens to also appreciate in price, and then receiving INC in the process.

However, there is no other real utility for INC token and time will tell if the price appreciation holds. Some criticism is that being inflationary (albeit technically disinflationary), it's a token that faces sell pressure constantly as users farm and take INC profits. Although it has the lowest supply of all four tokens, it's also the most inflationary.

Pulsechain Architecture

Pulsechain has a similar architecture to Ethereum given that it is a fork and copy of all the Ethereum source code. However, there are some key differences in the way Pulsechain has been implemented. Whereas Ethereum has many validators owned by centralized entities such as Kraken and Lido, this is not the case for Pulsechain. The community has set up over 50,000 validators at the time of writing. Only Ethereum currently has more validators and Pulsechain has way more than other chains such as Solana, which has about 3000. As a result, Pulsechain makes a great claim for decentralization given the large number of validators and that none are owned by centralized entities. This also means that the apy that validators earn (currently 9.5%) goes to the validators, with no other entity taking a cut. The protocol pays out the full apy. In Ethereum however, users can receive apy by staking on centralized exchanges where those entities take a cut of that apy for their service. However, in theory at least, there is also no absolute guarantee the apy will be paid as those entities have control. If those entities have any financial issues, who knows if the payments could be delayed or never paid at all. On the other hand, it's an extra feature that Ethereum offers as it pays rewards with less effort, but for decentralization purists they likely will resist the idea.

Although, the mechanism of staking and the validation process is essentially the same as Ethereum, for the sake of completeness and a recap, the following describes the operation of Pulsechain validators and rewards. This may also add some extra information not mentioned in the Ethereum chapter.

32 validators are chosen at random for each epoch to be a block proposer, thus proposing a block for each slot, where validators receive **proposal rewards** on success. As the number of validators in the system increases, the probability of being chosen as block proposer decreases. Therefore, as a form of compensation, the rewards for proposing a block are higher than attestations.

In each epoch, there is a committee of validators allocated to each of the 32 slots that partake in Pulsechain consensus where they vote on the validity of the block for that slot. In the process, Pulsechain validators earn **attestation rewards**. These rewards are paid in the next epoch, and it should be noted that these tend to be the lowest paid rewards compared to the others. Every validator shares its vote with the committee for each epoch and these votes all combine into one attestation. This one attestation is an aggregation of all signatures into one signature representing all validators who agree with the data.

An attestation consists of the following components:

Aggregation Bits: A list representing validators, where each entry contains a validator index, indicating whether they signed the data meaning they agree with the proposer of the block.

Data: Details related to the attestation, including:

- Slot number
- Committee index (committee id for the validator for a slot)
- Head of the attested block
- Source and target checkpoints
- Signature: A signature that aggregates each signature for a validator

There are also **sync-committee rewards**, where there is a group of 512 validators selected at random to sign block headers for each slot. Light clients use these headers where they can validate blocks without having to download the entire blockchain. The sync-committee is refreshed every 256 epochs. This reward, however, is less than the block proposal reward.

The following illustrates the Pulsechain architecture where a validator, selected by the committee, proposes a block for a given slot in the epoch:

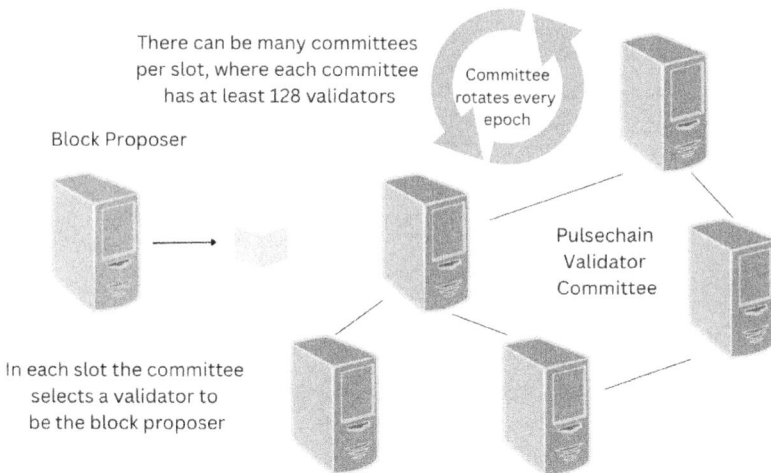

IPFS on Pulsechain

To make the whole ecosystem as decentralized as possible the team have changed many of the websites to now use IPFS. These websites are the Pulsechain block explorer, the PulseX DEX and the Pulsechain bridge.

IPFS stands for Inter Planetary File System. It's a decentralized and peer to peer protocol for storing and sharing files in a distributed network. Standard websites using HTTP use location-based addressing, but IPFS uses content-based addressing. IPFS is addressed by its contents, not its location, by using a CID (Content Identifier) which is a unique string with a hash of the data. The problem with location-based addressing is that it's prone to attack because the servers can be attacked based on the location, and it also has a central point of failure if the servers go offline. However, on the other hand, a user must download software to use IPFS if they want to get the most out of it, which requires a little extra knowledge and mindset shift compared to using a standard web browser.

The following illustrates how IPFS compares to HTTP location-based approach. The IPFS nodes wear the hat of a server and a client:

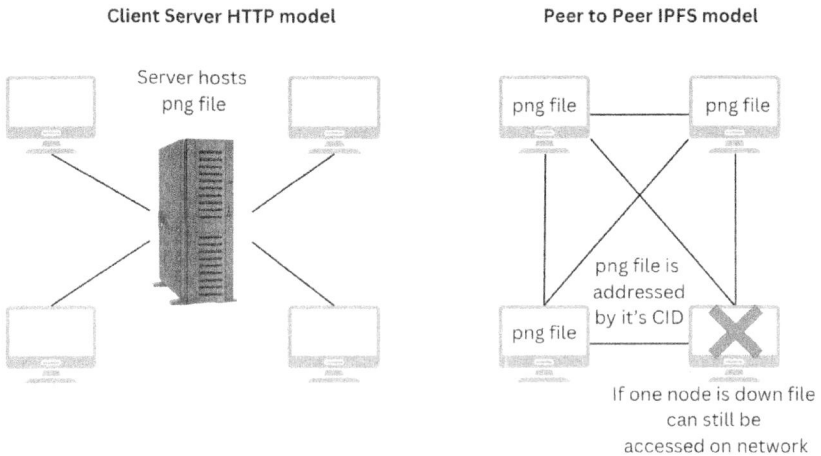

Client Server HTTP model

Server hosts png file

Peer to Peer IPFS model

png file — png file

png file is addressed by it's CID

png file

If one node is down file can still be accessed on network

184

The Pros of IPFS are:

- Less centralization risk compared to location-based addressing
- Less prone to attack compared to location-based addressing
- The focus shifts from where the data resides to what the data contains, thus increasing security
- Increased censorship resistance due to its peer-to-peer nature

The Cons of IPFS are:

- There is some complexity in managing the CIDs
- Users need to download IPFS software and understand CIDs, so there is a learning curve. The alternative is to use an IPFS gateway, where no software needs to be downloaded. This allows the user to use a regular web browser to access IPFS content, but this increases centralization risk, which goes against the decentralized nature of what IPFS intends to achieve.
- It provides transport encryption, so data is protected when being sent from one node to another. However, it doesn't provide content encryption by default, so extra protection must be provided to encrypt any files before adding to IPFS if there is any sensitive data.

In relation to the Pulsechain ecosystem each website for Pulsechain, for example the PulseX DEX (app.pulsex.com), has a button that navigates to the traditional HTTP website via the IPFS gateway. However, to use IPFS with its true intention there is also a set of buttons that allow the user to download the software for the respective operating system.

The following illustrates how the PulseX DEX works with IPFS:

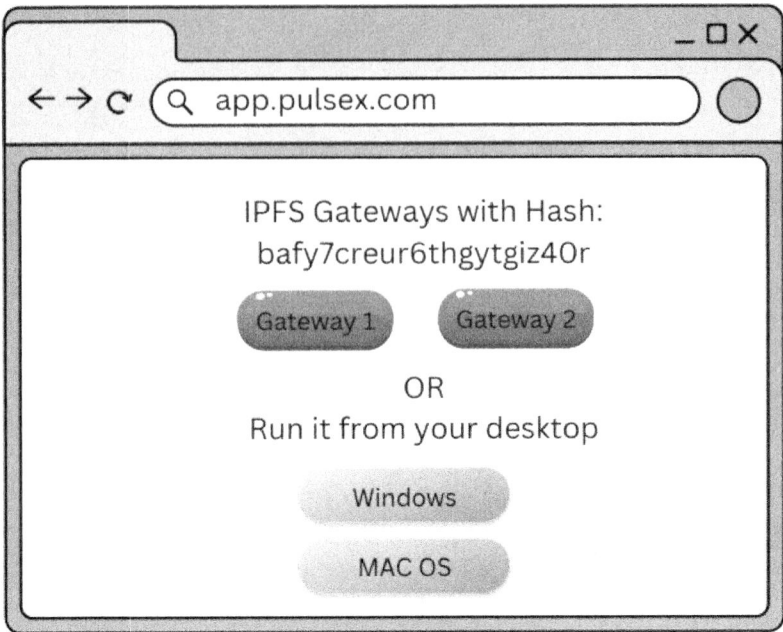

In the illustration the buttons for the IPFS gateways (Gateway 1 and Gateway 2) take the user to the traditional HTTP website. It provides a hash (which the CID is based on) that the gateways relate to. This is important because a different hash will produce a different CID. The hash referenced on the website is the one that has the true content that contains the PulseX logic. It also provides the option for the user to download the IPFS software for Windows or MAC (the actual site provides more options, but for simplicity two buttons are listed in the picture).

Due to the peer to peer and decentralized nature of IPFS, this provides Pulsechain with yet another layer of protection in that it makes it much more difficult for any entity to shut down the use of the Pulsechain blockchain. This is because although a Pulsechain website can be shut down, a peer-to-peer IPFS network, for the most part, cannot be, thus increasing censorship resistance, a core principle for blockchain technology.

In summary, Pulsechain prides itself on having decentralization as a core property for its ecosystem. In addition to 50,000 validators providing a high level of decentralization, IPFS brings Pulsechain to another level of decentralization which is currently unique compared to other blockchains.

Pulsechain's incentive mechanism

Pulsechain has a very interesting and unique incentive mechanism to drive adoption and fulfil pillars of the trilemma such as Decentralization. Later in the book the Saito blockchain also has a completely different and unique approach to getting adoption and incentivizing its users to run nodes and keep the network decentralized by making sure that all node types are rewarded, not just miners or validators. Pulsechain however, uses a very different approach mainly based on game theory and other interesting incentives.

Faster and Cheaper fees

For the first part, Pulsechain is a cheaper and faster version of Ethereum. Some would argue that it wasn't built from the ground up. Others would say this is a genius approach because it took the most known and adopted smart contract platform and aimed to improve it with superior game theory. From that angle, one could say it's a better version of Ethereum, albeit unproven to some extent because it's much newer. Therefore, one attraction for adoption and onboarding new users, being existing Ethereum users or elsewhere, is the cheaper fees and faster speed (albeit just 17% faster, but faster nonetheless).

Low cost to setup validators

Secondly, setting up a Pulsechain validator requires 32,000,000 PLS, similar in concept to Ethereum where 32 ETH is required. However, the difference being PLS is much cheaper in dollar terms than ETH. At the time of writing, setting up a Pulsechain validator costs about $3000 (it was as low as $1000 when the majority were set up) compared to about $110,000 for Ethereum! This is yet another driver for decentralization and adoption. The evidence is clear in that Pulsechain currently has 50,000 validators, more than any other smart contract blockchain except Ethereum itself, in part because it's a cheaper setup. The price of PLS was zero on launch, as those who sacrificed prior to launch received an airdrop at $0. After this it was around $0.0001 on average for many months, therefore allowing the community to set up validators cheaply. This contrasts with Ethereum because since its move to PoS the price of ETH was still very high, making it difficult for users to host their own validator, thus creating a system where many entities with deeper pockets such as Kraken and Lido control large amounts of staked ETH.

Free copy of all ERC 20 tokens

On launch all ERC 20 tokens were copied to Pulsechain as part of its full stateful fork. This allows Liquidity Providers to pair these free copies with the ERC 20 version. For example, a Liquidity Provider can bridge over LINK tokens from Ethereum (called eLINK) and pair them with the free copy, the PRC-20 token (called pLINK). The pLINK tokens were airdropped on launch at $0, therefore allowing providers to set up one side of the pair for the pool effectively for free. This is a unique piece of game theory as traditionally Liquidity Pools require a pair of tokens where the provider needs to buy a certain amount of each side of the pair to set up the pool. For example, pairing ETH with LINK on Ethereum requires some ETH and some LINK (in the simple case 50% are ETH tokens and the other 50% are LINK tokens). However, if the provider decides to provide liquidity where one side of the pair was a free airdropped PRC-20 token then this creates a cheaper way to set up liquidity pools, possibly attracting attention and therefore adoption, from other ecosystems. This also leads to more transactions and buying and burning of PLSX token and burning of PLS itself, which is positive for the main native ecosystem tokens too.

It remains to be seen if this piece of game theory really takes off because it is somewhat of an experiment. Many of the free PRC-20 tokens may not work natively on Pulsechain unless developers for those tokens decide to build on Pulsechain. However, that doesn't stop people speculating on those tokens and ratio trading. It can be seen as a positive either way because this proves the Pulsechain teams' approach to innovation and experimentation to push the boundaries.

Heart's Law

There is a concept created by the founder called Heart's law. The fine details of liquidity pools are outside the scope of this book, but the idea is that prices of assets that trade against each other move with each other because the liquidity bonds them in the trading pair. Therefore, if one side of the pair moves up in price it essentially pulls up the other side of the pair with it. This is a large part of the reason why the market tends to move up when BTC or ETH move up because BTC and ETH are widely used as pairs in liquidity pools.

Let's look at an example of how this can happen.

In the simple case (with Uniswap v1 pools) there is a requirement that the value of both assets in the pair are the same on both sides of the pool. In a later version of Uniswap they introduced concentrated liquidity pools where this was not a pre-requisite, but for the sake of simplicity we can assume equal amounts. The result is the same effect either way.

If we have 10 ETH at $5000 each in a liquidity pool that holds 1000 units of Coin B at $50 each where for simplicity, this is the only liquidity pool for this coin.

In liquidity pools there is this formula:

(number of Token A) * (price of Token A) = (number of Token B) * (price of Token B)

Now let's assume no trades on this pair have occurred but, in the market, ETH has appreciated in price 10%. Remember that the value of both sides of the pool must be the same:

(10 ETH) * ($5500) = (1000 Coin B) * (X)

(10 * $5500) / (1000) = X

X = $55

The value of Coin B is now $55, so it has also gone up 10%, which adheres to the formula.

This can all relate back to the free PRC 20 tokens in that if these are used in liquidity pools then these free copies could also drive up in value due to Heart's law. For example, in a pool with eLINK (the bridged over LINK from Ethereum) and pLINK tokens, the pLINK token (which is the free copy) price can be pulled up if the value of eLINK increases.

Summary and Pulsechain statistics

In summary, only one year after launch Pulsechain is currently number 8 by TVL (Total Value Locked) out of all Layer 1 blockchains on DefiLlama (a website that tracks on chain statistics), out of about 250 blockchains!

The PulseX DEX is also about number 8 by TVL, out of 1000 DEXs! Although PulseX only runs on its native chain, Pulsechain, the other DEXs run on many other chains. For example, Uniswap runs on 14 chains and SushiSwap runs on 32 chains. So, on a per chain comparison basis this puts PulseX at number 3.

The number of daily transactions is about 400,000 on Pulsechain, ranking it number 10. Based on these numbers, Pulsechain certainly seems to be gaining traction and adoption and this could well be because of its strong incentive mechanism outlined in this section.

Potential Upcoming Features

Single sided staking

Generally, in liquidity pools a pair of tokens are allocated, but the issue is that because one token in the pair is priced in terms of the other, it can lead to impermanent loss. Essentially this means that the liquidity provider loses money compared to holding the tokens outside of the pool (which is why they are compensated with the rewards). Had the provider just held the tokens outside the pool, they would have gained much more.

Single sided staking allows users to stake a single token and receive rewards. There is no token priced in terms of the other, so this alleviates impermanent loss. This is much less risky. The only risk is smart contract risk which applies to the whole cryptocurrency space and smart contracts anyway.

Single sided staking would be provided in the PulseX DEX, where there is currently a screen and button for this, but it does nothing for now. Users could lock the PLSX token and earn rewards in other tokens. The other tokens would be a set of tokens that the user can choose to earn rewards in. They would be in a pre-defined list. The idea is that a new project on Pulsechain that wants to promote itself can be listed as a token to earn rewards when staking PLSX. This list of tokens would be chosen from a vote likely by PLSX holders.

Single sided staking simplifies the process because only a single token is required compared to maintaining two tokens in a pool. In liquidity pools, there is a price range that is initially set and if the pool goes outside that range, the provider needs to change the range to reflect the new price. This is not the case with single sided staking. There are no ratios to maintain as there is only one token.

This mechanism also reduces the available supply of a token, in this case PLSX, which given the same or more demand, results in a higher price for PLSX itself. The rewards earned can then also be traded or staked in farms to earn more rewards, essentially turning the ecosystem into one huge yield farm!

At present, there is no guarantee this feature will be implemented and exactly how it will work, but again it shows the innovation and nature of the team where they are not afraid to experiment and try new ideas and push boundaries.

Tokenomics

Since a large part and a significant strength of Pulsechain is its game theory and tokenomics, this chapter has already covered this in depth. However, let's recap the tokenomics of the four main tokens in the Pulsechain ecosystem created by the Pulsechain team as a summary.

The tokens **PLS** and **PLSX** are both deflationary. PLS has an extra 25% burned with each transaction compared to ETH on Ethereum, and PLSX gets bought up and burned with each transaction on the PulseX DEX.

The **Incentive Token (INC)** is paid as a reward to Liquidity Providers who can stake their LP tokens earned in the pool to earn even more rewards in the form of INC. Those who have tokens in farms can also earn INC. This token is inflationary, but the inflation reduces over time.

HEX was copied from Ethereum, and this allowed users to lock up HEX to earn yield. Each user earns more yield (in HEX) if they lock bigger and longer. However, the lower the amount of HEX locked out of the total HEX supply in the system, the higher the individual yield for each user that locks HEX. HEX inflates at 3.69% per year but since only about 10% of all HEX is locked in total, this means users can get up to 36.9% apy depending on how much is locked and for how long. Any attempt to unlock the HEX before the lockup period chosen results in a penalty that is paid to all other users that locked their tokens.

References

The following links provide more detail on the Pulsechain ecosystem and how to use it:

The official Pulsechain website:

https://pulsechain.com/

The ultimate community resource for projects on Pulsechain, tools and everything you need to know such as the ecosystem, community and building on Pulsechain:

https://GoPulseChain.com

Pulsechain education for beginners and links to Pulsechain block explorer:

https://www.howtopulse.com/

Statistics for number of Pulsechain Validators, PLSX burned and other ecosystem stats:

https://gopulse.com/

Information on PulseX and providing liquidity:

https://www.howtopulse.com/how-to-add-liquidity-to-pulsex-a-guide-on-how-it-works/

Ecosystem walkthrough - how to buy PLS and PLSX, using the Pulsechain bridge and statistics websites:

https://drive.google.com/file/d/1ze9B3yim37pwM9W5mrlKDVA_ZyRaKSXH/view

Sei

Brief History

Sei was launched in August 2023 with an aim to address the "Exchange Trilemma" faced by decentralized exchanges where security, decentralization and liquidity need to be balanced and optimized. In the context of trading applications there is also a "Trading Trilemma" of scalability, capital efficiency and decentralization which Sei sought to solve. It has been designed to achieve a high number of transactions per second as part of the solution to this trilemma, in the order of 12500 to 20000 tps. As a result, Sei is particularly optimized for trading applications in addition to NFT marketplaces, DeFi and gaming applications where trading of assets occur.

Its approach uses unique innovations such as Twin Turbo consensus and market-based parallelization leading to high throughput, thereby looking to be a superior infrastructure for exchanges. This allows Sei to be an ideal platform for any trading application to perform better than other blockchain platforms as its approach is to optimize every layer of the stack, providing solid infrastructure for exchanges.

Sei utilizes the Cosmos SDK (Software Development Kit) and Tendermint framework and runs as part of the Cosmos ecosystem leveraging the Inter-Blockchain Communication (IBC) protocol, allowing it to interoperate with many other blockchains in the Cosmos network. The Cosmos SDK, Tendermint framework and IBC are outside the scope of this book, but the References section in this chapter delves into this in more detail.

What Problem is Sei Trying to Solve?

In the cryptocurrency sphere, there are a variety of use cases, but it can be said indisputably that trading is by far the most adopted use case. This is where Sei enters the space, being a specialized blockchain platform for trading which has introduced new improvements in transaction processing, block propagation and parallelization.

Most people in the blockchain arena tend to think that DeFi is the only application used for trading, but trading of assets also occurs in gaming applications and NFTs. The ability to exchange assets in many contexts is crucial, not just on decentralized exchanges.

There are many challenges with existing blockchain trading applications such as scalability and reliability and this prevents mass adoption. The **exchange trilemma** is a problem most crypto exchanges struggle with where this refers to maximizing security, decentralization and liquidity all together. Most exchanges optimize two of the three facets of this trilemma while trading off the other. Centralized exchanges treat liquidity and security with a higher priority but this trades off decentralization. A decentralized exchange prioritizes decentralization and security with the cost of lower liquidity, and this affects users trading effectively without incurring slippage (a variation of the intended buy or sell price).

Sei solves the exchange trilemma by optimizing all three facets. In particular, it uses **Frequent Batch Auctioning** to optimize the security component of the Exchange Trilemma. It mitigates front running risk by aggregating all market orders and executing them at a uniform clearing price. This prevents validators from placing orders in a certain way to maximize profit for themselves, a form of MEV (maximal extractable value). For example, if transactions are executed sequentially a validator can view an incoming order and then place a buy order before the incoming transaction is processed and then a sell order after it to sell at a higher price.

In terms of the liquidity facet of the Exchange Trilemma, Sei has implemented **Native Order Books** which are built directly on its blockchain. There is a matching engine which allows exchanges to build on Sei so they can deploy their own order books. This leads to decentralized apps on Sei accessing a shared liquidity pool resulting in deeper liquidity (all on chain), therefore leading to less price slippage and tighter spreads.

The key to these order books is that Sei (based on Tendermint framework) has a built-in centralized limit order book (CLOB). A CLOB is an order book where the buy and sell orders are managed by a central body and this approach has been used in the traditional markets, such as the stock market, for the last few decades. It is a very centralized framework however, and based on web2 technology, rather than the newer web3 decentralized technology in blockchain, hence this approach has only been adopted on Centralized Exchanges (CEXs) for cryptocurrency.

This is where a newer decentralized approach using AMMs (Automated Market Makers) came into the scene such as Uniswap for example. This allowed the ability for any user to create their own trading pairs and provide liquidity into a pool for that pair (for example ETH, LINK). In this decentralized approach there is more flexibility and options available. There is no explicit order book with buyers and sellers but rather a pool of tokens for the pair that users can add or remove from the pool depending on which token of the pair they are buying. The disadvantage with AMMs is that they are less efficient than CLOBs because they have higher price slippage (due to less liquidity) and give potential rise to front running where traders can manipulate prices by viewing incoming orders. This is where Sei arises on the scene, bringing a novel approach where there is a blockchain purposely built for a CLOB approach to reside on it with specific optimizations.

Bringing CLOBs onto the Sei blockchain

A CLOB requires a stable infrastructure, high speed and low cost, all of which are enabled by Sei's platform. Some of the optimizations are described in the "Sei's Consensus Mechanism" section, later in this chapter, which details approaches for transaction processing and block propagation. However, there are a few other optimizations and features to mention that allow deep liquidity and better price matching for applications and traders.

Native Price Oracles allow validators to maintain and provide accurate price information to make sure prices are always intact and prices are kept up to date with a voting window. This is done by the validators who play a dual role in consensus and as an oracle to provide asset pricing. Validators must submit their price data within the voting window to ensure accurate information.

Another innovation is Sei processes order book transactions (buy and sell orders) at the end of a block to prevent front running and market fairness. When orders are aggregated at the end of a block, Sei makes sure that transactions are executed in parallel rather than in sequence meaning that all trades are matched at the same time and therefore traders cannot act on information before other traders. This results in a uniform clearing price as all participants in the system receive the same price. This is Frequent Batch Auctioning (FBA), explained briefly earlier. Usually, the way for a participant to front run transactions is to pay a higher gas fee so they can get their transaction in the block before others, but since front running is now mitigated this also lowers gas costs. This in turn improves liquidity as now more orders can be filled at once.

In summary, Sei brings the benefits of CLOBs on to the blockchain in a decentralized manner effectively combining the best facets of AMMs and CLOBs.

Sei's Consensus Mechanism

Sei uses a unique approach known as **Twin Turbo Consensus** in conjunction with PoS whereby in addition to validators proposing voting on blocks based on the amount of SEI tokens they hold; twin turbo consensus then achieves rapid finality involving a two-round process where validators vote on the proposed block to either accept or reject it.

Twin Turbo Consensus optimizes both the block propagation and block processing phases, hence the name "twin turbo". Sei also leverages the Tendermint Consensus framework in Cosmos where it can use single slot finality essentially meaning that when a block is added to the chain, it is considered final. Once finalized, the transactions in the block cannot be reversed, therefore achieving instant finality which is an important component of scalability of transactions. Sei's finality time is about 300ms.

To grasp the background of how Twin Turbo consensus emerged, let's first understand which component of the lifecycle of transactions occupy the majority of consensus:

- Creating a Transaction and Initialization (almost zero seconds)
- Submitting transactions to the Mempool (Can be 1 or more seconds and varies a lot)
- Proposing a Block (almost zero seconds)
- Voting and Building Blocks (about 12 seconds)
- Finalizing Blocks (from a few minutes to a few hours)

It's clear that finalizing blocks is a large portion of consensus. However, the Tendermint framework allows single slot finality and therefore instant finality of transactions, so for Sei, this becomes negligible, partly also because Sei labs were able to push time limits of the Tendermint Framework and reduce block times and finality times significantly. Note that the current finality time of 300 ms (not completely instant) is due to extra cryptographic processing that Sei carries out as part of its Twin Turbo mechanism. In the bigger picture, this is still quite negligible, especially when compared to other blockchains.

The next component is the voting and constructing of blocks, as the others are all very negligible. This is where Twin Turbo makes a difference, which consists of two parts that have been optimized, block processing and block propagation. These were optimized in the Tendermint stack.

The first optimization, block propagation, has been optimized using **Intelligent Block Propagation** to make sure blocks are transferred more efficiently. Prior to this optimization a proposer of a block initially creates a block with transactions which is then sent across the network to other validators. Once they receive this block proposal, they must wait to obtain the complete block containing critical information so that the contents can be verified, after which they can then proceed with consensus and link the block to the chain. When a node receives a transaction however, it's broadcast to many other nodes which means there is a lot of redundant data transmitted because validators (most of the time) already have transactions in their local mempool where they can build a block locally.

Sei optimizes this by reducing the "wait time" for the complete block. Rather than sending the entire block, a compact block proposal containing transaction identifiers and a reference to the full block is sent instead. This is done in the following way:

- Block proposers send the proposal to other validators. This is sent as a single message.
- The entire block consisting of the full contents of each transaction is then sent. However, the full block is not sent in one piece, but rather broken into smaller sections and gossiped to other validators in a random fashion. This allows packets to travel faster in the network and

allows these smaller parts to be processed in parallel, increasing throughput.

- If a validator already has the transactions it requires, it can rebuild the full block without waiting for the smaller parts of the block to be received. Validators may already have these transactions due to the gossiping step earlier.
- If a validator doesn't have the transactions it needs, it waits for the block's full contents to be received before reconstructing the block. Thus, the act of waiting is only required in this situation, resulting in up to a 40% throughput increase.

The following illustrates the above steps for a situation where the validator does not have transactions in its local mempool and for the other situation when it does. You can see that validator A has gossiped transactions to validator B, so validator B already has them in its mempool:

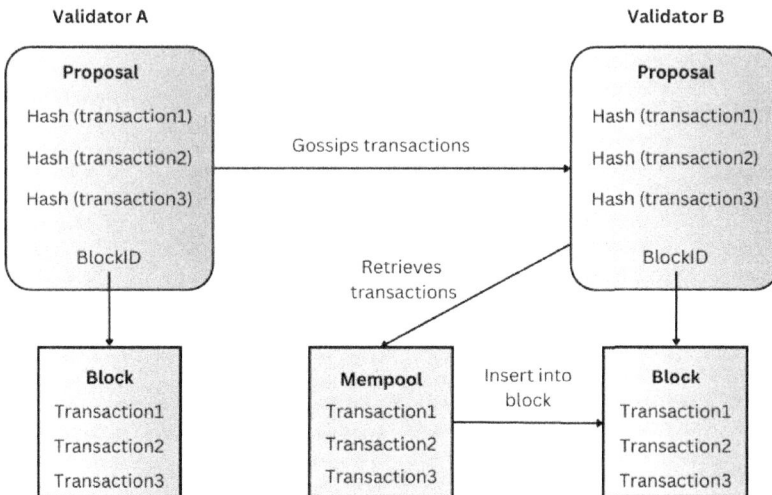

The second optimization, block processing has been optimized using **Optimistic Block Processing** where essentially there is a mechanism that handles blocks in such a way that assumes they will be accepted.

In the Tendermint consensus, once a block proposal is received by a validator, it verifies that the block is valid and then progresses to two steps call pre-vote and pre-commit. In essence these two steps are consensus rule checks that must be passed for a block to be accepted, thus it's a pre-check to make sure validators don't reject the block later due to failing the block validation rules.

However, with the optimization, instead of waiting for the pre-commit and pre-vote steps to complete before processing transactions, the validators run a process in parallel to optimistically process the first block at a certain height. The state is then written to cache memory (a temporary fast access memory store), and if that block gets accepted by validators, then the data from the cache is committed. If it's not accepted, then the data in the cache is discarded and any future runs for that block height will not use optimistic processing.

The reason for this whole approach is that usually the first proposed block is the one that is accepted after the voting phase and so Sei takes advantage of this high probability. This optimization in conjunction with Optimistic Block Propagation renders fast finality and high scalability that is critical in trading applications.

How Transaction Parallelization works

In addition to Optimistic Block Processing there is another aspect of parallel processing, being parallel processing of transactions themselves. Instead of processing transactions in a sequential fashion, Sei can process them in parallel to increase performance. Data is stored in **key-value pairs** where essentially a **key** is a unique identifier for some data and the **value** is the data itself. However, there may be dependencies (where things need to happen in a certain order) between keys so messages updating the same key will need to be run sequentially but messages that update different keys can be run in parallel. So, before transactions in a block are executed, the dependencies between each of these transactions are built using a Direct Acyclic Graph (DAG) which contains the different resources (indexed by a key) that messages in each transaction must use.

The following illustrates this mechanism, where there are messages that update certain keys. A DAG is constructed that shows the dependency mapping. Based on this, it can be decided which updates can be done in sequence and which can be done in parallel:

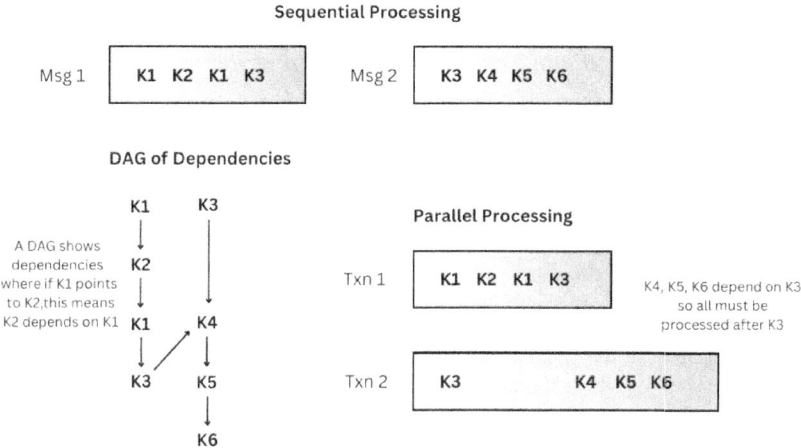

Note that a DAG of dependencies show arrows where for example if K1 has an arrow pointing to K2, this means that K2 depends on K1, or must be processed after K1.

You can see in Message1 (Msg1) it updates the same keys (K1), so this must be processed sequentially. K3 can be processed in parallel but the subsequent keys (K4, K5 and K6) all depend on K3 so must be processed after K3.

Since PoS has largely been covered in this book, in the interest of not being repetitive, this chapter won't delve more into this. Essentially, think of Sei's consensus mechanism as PoS with Twin Turbo for optimizing the consensus approach.

Sei vs Ethereum

One key difference and selling point for Sei is its ability to process transactions and smart contracts in parallel, but Ethereum operates sequentially. As a concept, those familiar with programming understand single threading and multi-threading. In a multi-threaded environment, different paths of codes can run at the same time. A lock can protect access to shared resources, which otherwise may be corrupted (if two threads of code try to access a shared resource at the same time). This is all in the context of code running on a single processor, but a similar concept exists for access to shared resources across many processors, which is a multi-processor environment. At a high-level think of Sei operating as a similar concept to this.

Also, note that Sei uses single slot finality. This is very important to understand as every epoch has many slots. Ethereum has 32 slots in an epoch but the blocks for those slots are not finalized per slot, but rather at the end of the epoch (two rounds for Ethereum). Sei achieves finality at the end of a slot.

This following table summarizes some key differences between Sei and Ethereum:

	Sei	Ethereum
TTF (Time to Finality)	300ms to 600ms using single slot finality.	13 to 15 minutes
Front running prevention and order books	Built into the protocol natively.	Not built into the protocol natively
Smart contract and transaction processing	Parallel. Some must be done sequentially depending on the ordering and resources that messages have.	Sequential. Each transaction must wait for the previous one to be completed before execution.
Scalability approach	Twin Turbo Consensus, Optimistic Processing and Intelligent Block Propagation.	Danksharding and other layer 2s such as rollups.
Current number of transactions per second	30 – 50. More with Sei v2 upgrade and possible maximum of 28,300.	15 – 30. Likely much more with Full Danksharding and Layer 2s, about 100,000 tps.

Sei's Order Book Architecture

Sei's orderbooks have been specialized and built into its main layer. This section shows a comparison with Solana's orderbook architecture which is built on the application layer (or layer 2). Sei's architecture is shown in the following diagram:

Layer 2 applications

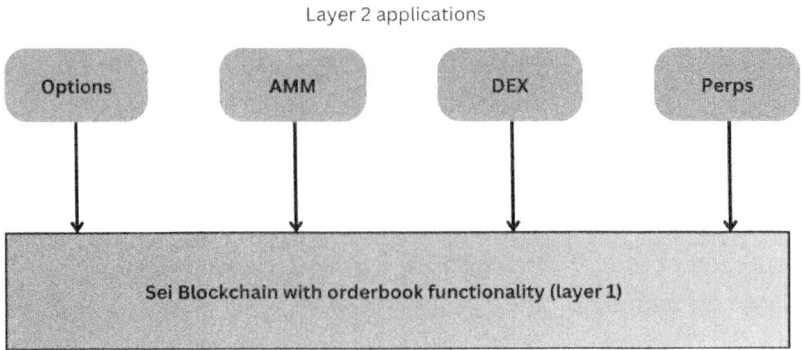

Solana is a general-purpose chain and the orderbook is built at layer 2, so its architecture has the disadvantage of competing resources such as gaming apps that contribute to congestion on the chain. Solana's architecture is shown below:

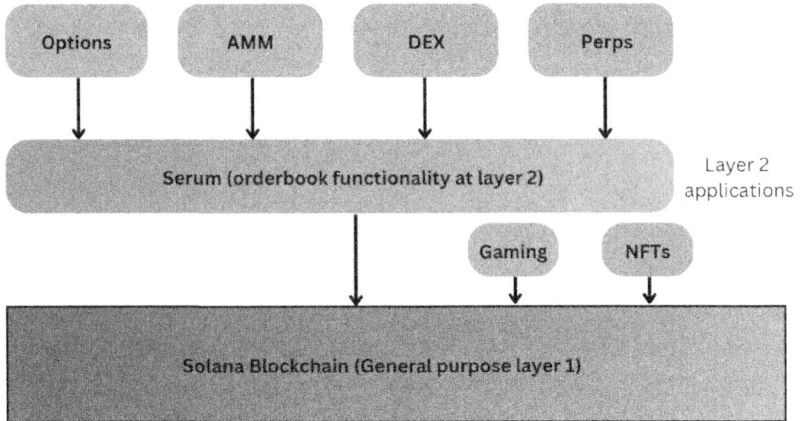

Upcoming Features and Upgrades

The main upcoming upgrade for Sei is Sei v2. Sei currently has different software components that interact to support the chain. Some of these components interact with the consensus layer, and others interact with the execution layer. The upgrade changes the execution layer to support optimistic parallelization. This will contain the following features and upgrades with the end goal being a fully parallelized EVM:

Optimistic parallelization: Parallelization so that developers won't require dependencies where they need to define the state access themselves. Rather, the chain will optimistically run transactions in parallel and track the areas of storage that a transaction interacts with. If a transaction interacts with different areas of storage they are run again in parallel, but those interacting with the same area of storage are run in sequence. So, in summary, although Sei currently supports a form of parallelization (already covered in this chapter), this is an extra optimization to make sure that if a transaction interacts with the same state, essentially a conflict, then it keeps track of the parts of storage each transaction is interacting with.

EVM smart contract backward compatibility: This allows developers to deploy smart contracts from other EVM compatible blockchains without requiring extra changes. Currently, developers need to rewrite smart contracts and deploy them on Sei. However, with v2 backwards compatibility, any significant smart contract on Ethereum can deployed easily on Sei. This also assists with existing tools like Metamask as all the user needs to do is change the RPC connection to point to the Sei chain.

Batched transactions of 28300 per second: This is a major performance enhancement due to the parallelization updates mentioned.

Tokenomics

The native token of Sei Network is SEI. The total supply of SEI tokens is capped at 10 billion. The token serves multiple functions within the network, including paying for transaction fees, staking for network security, participating in governance, and acting as native asset liquidity or collateral for applications built on Sei. About half of the SEI token supply was allocated to the community to support ecosystem initiatives and staking rewards.

Initial launch and token distribution

On initial launch 18% of the SEI tokens were in circulation meaning that another 82% are yet to unlock which makes the behavior inflationary in nature.

The distribution of Sei tokens is as below:

Ecosystem Reserve: 48% (for staking rewards and other ecosystem initiatives)

Team: 20%

Private Sale Investors: 20%

Foundation: 9%

Launchpool: 3% (for community participation)

SEI token utility

SEI tokens are used for paying transaction fees and users can pay a tip to validators if they want to prioritize their transactions in the queue, ensuring efficiency. Also, SEI can be used as trading fees where exchanges that run on its chain charge a trading fee for swaps, and that fee is paid in SEI tokens.

SEI holders can partake in the PoS consensus mechanism by running a node or delegating their stake to another validator. They can also be used as part of governance of the system which helps to shape the future of the blockchain as it evolves.

Final Thoughts

Sei appears to have a bright future, especially considering it as a parallelized EVM as this brings interoperability and parallel processing, something not all blockchains possess. It could be said as a specialized blockchain for trading that perhaps DEXs and DEX aggregators could catch up in terms of speed and liquidity as they constantly improve.

The future of DEXs and DEX aggregators appears to be promising as they are expected to continue improving decentralized trading by offering users a smoother trading experience, especially in terms of finding the best prices and reducing costs.

However, the specialized nature of Sei as an order book DEX environment renders a competitive edge, especially for traders who prioritize speed and control over their trades. Sei has very unique features, such as frontrunning protection and the native order-matching engine which provide a tailored experience and likely will continue to attract a specific segment of the market.

So, although DEX aggregators are likely to evolve and potentially match the liquidity and speed offered by specialized environments like Sei, its focused approach on order book trading will likely maintain its relevance. Both roles are important, and their coexistence provides traders with a choice based on their specific requirements and trading styles.

References

The following links provide more detail on the Sei ecosystem:

Official site with information on twin turbo consensus, transactions per second, community, Sei block explorer, details for developers and blogs:

https://www.sei.io/

Sei whitepaper:

https://github.com/sei-protocol/sei-chain/blob/main/whitepaper/Sei_Whitepaper.pdf

Sei Block explorer:

https://www.seiscan.app/pacific-1

Information on the Tendermint Framework, Cosmos SDK and IBC:

https://tendermint.com/

Information on Sei v2:

https://blog.sei.io/sei-v2-the-first-parallelized-evm/

Emerging Blockchains with Different Consensus

Saito

Brief History

Saito was conceptualized by David Lancashire and Richard Parris in the spring of 2017. The goal was to create a blockchain that could solve the trilemma by achieving scalability without trading off decentralization or security.

The whitepaper described its original approach to consensus and transaction processing. The consensus mechanism is Proof-of-Routing Work, where nodes are rewarded based on transactions they validate and broadcast rather than the usual PoW or PoS methods.

What problem is Saito solving?

As mentioned earlier, Saito, like most other blockchains, aims to solve the trilemma using a unique consensus approach, Proof of Routing Work. Before we delve into the consensus mechanism let's take a higher-level view of what the real problem is. In summary, all blockchains maintain their security using mining or validating by allocating a security budget which rewards miners and validators for securing the network. On the surface, this appears all well because security, especially where money is involved, is extremely important. However, as described in the Trilemma section at the beginning of this book, this leads to trading off decentralization and scalability. Some blockchains such as Kadena and Kaspa, appear to have solved this, or at least that's what they have claimed. But what if the problem isn't a technological problem? Or what if the problem is partly a technological problem? That doesn't fully address the problem overall. Perhaps, as Saito claims, backed with evidence to support this (more on this later), the problem is an economic issue. It may well be a technological issue as well, but Saito has addressed both with their solution.

It is clear from other blockchains in general that the majority have scalability issues, or if not centralization issues where security is largely intact. This is because there is a security budget that rewards miners and validators, thus being incentivized to secure the blockchain. However, there is no budget or incentive to keep the blockchain decentralized or scalable in that there are no rewards to nodes for this.

The Free Rider Problem

The first real issue is known as the "Free Rider Problem" of economics. The free-rider problem is the burden on a shared resource that is created by its use or overuse by people who aren't paying their fair share for it or aren't paying anything at all.

This problem arises in blockchains because payments are distributed to one type of work, being mining or staking, but not other types of work such as routing transactions. This imbalance creates a misalignment of incentives where users maximize their spending on work they are paid for and minimize it on any other kind of work. Essentially this results in those users who pay for the unpaid work subsidizing the miners and stakers, which is fine while volunteers are happy to continue but eventually this dries up, especially at scale. The miners and stakers are therefore free riding on those doing the unpaid work such as fee collection or application development.

In general, many blockchains attempt to solve this issue by making certain operations more exclusive which increases scalability but destroys the openness of the network. Saito has a different approach, as you will find in this chapter.

The Tragedy of the Commons

This is an economic problem where the individual consumes a resource at the expense of society. If an individual acts in their best interest, it can result in harm and excess consumption to the detriment of others and can result in total depletion of a shared resource.

An example would be over-fishing, where fishing grounds are open to all, individual fishermen have an incentive to catch as many fish as possible. However, if each fisherman catches fish for his own gain, the fish population can completely decline. Other examples are deforestation and air pollution.

In the context of blockchain, one common issue of depletion is the blockchain itself which bloats to a point where it becomes too large and expensive to host and can reduce transaction times and increase fees.

Also, the cost of running a node can be very large especially where there are large amounts of data (due to smart contracts for example) or the blockchain having a very long history (one that isn't pruned). That data must be stored somewhere, and this becomes a big problem if that data is to be hosted because most actors will not want to do that for free. Since hosting nodes is expensive with no incentives, the validators on Ethereum receiving the most rewards do not host public facing nodes. Instead, a centralized entity called Infura, hosts a large majority of the Ethereum nodes used for its transactions. To make this profitable one must control data on the network or charge extra fees on transactions for going through Infura (which is where part of the Metamask fees go to). The problem is that this results in a single entity acting as a gateway for the majority of Ethereum which is not in the best interests for decentralization.

Collusion of miners and selfish mining

Miners can play with information to be more competitive, and one way is hoarding transaction information, keeping lucrative transactions to themselves so others can't earn the fees.

Another tactic, called "selfish mining", is where a group of miners collude together to get a head-start on mining a fresh block and undermine the rest of the network. These tactics are a way to maximize profits in Proof of Work consensus mechanisms. Some debate whether this is purely academic or not. However, these exploits in the system allow those with the power to abuse them, and this means the collusion of large groups pooling their power collectively and using their power to earn more fees. The most successful groups are the most centralized ones. There is a reference to Selfish Mining in the References section of this chapter.

In summary, mining and staking is incentivized but the sharing and hosting of the data is not. Therefore, for the nodes to seriously make money the miners must either act and collude together in a group or monetize their services through a centralized entity such as Infura.

This all leads to a demise in scalability and decentralization, or certainly a huge challenge because it starts to trend to be more centralized as all the rewards centralize to the miner and validator nodes, but all the other nodes (non-mining) that participate in validating and broadcasting transactions receive no reward. How about they get rewarded? This is where Saito comes in!

Saito's Solution

Block Production

A large part of Saito's solution is the Proof of Routing Work consensus mechanism (now called Saito Consensus), whereby to produce a new block, the node proposing it must have accumulated a certain amount of "work", known as Routing Work. This work is a score based on a points system. A proposed block increases its Routing Work score by receiving transactions from other nodes and broadcasting that block. The fee included in the transaction determines the Routing Work whereby the first node to receive the fee gets a Routing Work score equal to the fee. Now the next set of remaining nodes that receives the transaction receive half the Routing Work points of what the first node received, and the next set after that gets half the points from the previous set, and this continues until all nodes have received the broadcasted transactions. Essentially, over the course of time nodes receive a proportional number of points and fees in relation to the amount of work they have done for the block that was accepted. However, to clarify the point score is reset with each block.

The blockchain maintains a "difficulty" for block production where this difficulty is measured in Routing Work. A node produces a block when it has sufficient routing work in the transactions mempool to meet this difficulty. If a block doesn't contain a sufficient routing work score, then this is invalid according to consensus rules.

Therefore, nodes not only have an incentive to accept transactions but to also propagate those transactions because this contributes to their work score. If the transaction isn't included in the block, they will not get credit for that, so this is why sharing transactions is important. So, propagating transactions as much and as quickly as possible is the work that subsidizes the network.

So, if nodes can collect transactions and fees from nodes that broadcast lots of transactions with high fees, this is beneficial because even though the work score and therefore fees halve each time, they can still collect those fees by accepting and sharing them. Sharing is now incentivized because if nodes cannot get the transaction into the next block, they cannot be eligible for any payment, but if they propagate the transaction to a node that succeeds in doing so, they now have eligibility for payment.

This solves the Free Rider problem because now incentives are not just aligned to the miners but all types of nodes, and they can all receive rewards for their activity. This means there is no situation where a node must be provisioned in an economically voluntary manner (which would then normally lead to having to host on a service such as Infura). This also solves the Collusion of Miners problem because sharing and hosting of data in Saito is incentivized.

The Golden Ticket and Payment Lottery

A known attack vector that has caused problems for PoS and PoW blockchains is "fee-recycling attack", which is a way for attackers to receive more rewards than they should even though they are doing the same amount of work as their peers. To prevent this, a payment lottery takes place.

The important thing to understand is that when a block is produced, it doesn't mean that node is instantly paid, but rather it means that node is eligible to be paid. Upon block production all the fees in the block are burned, so nobody is paid at this point. Miners then start hashing to find a "golden ticket" solution to solve the block that was produced. The golden ticket is a solution to a puzzle that upon being solved unlocks the funds for that block.

When a golden ticket is found a payout is issued worth the average fees burned per block. 50% of the fees are paid to the miner that found the golden ticket and the other 50% is paid statistically to the node that accumulated the greatest number of Routing Work points. To emphasize, a node that has done more Routing Work has a higher probability of receiving the reward, where the probability is proportional to the amount of work it has done. If a golden ticket is not found, no reward is paid to the miner at this point, but when the next golden ticket is found, any unpaid rewards are then paid to routers and stakers.

The way this lottery works is that there is a random number associated with the golden ticket. This is hashed to pick a random transaction from the previous block. The transaction has a higher chance of selection because it is weighted by its share of fees that contributed to the production of that block. The node is selected from the routing path of the winning transaction by hashing that number again. Each node's chance of selection is weighted according to the total amount of routing work held by all nodes at all points in that routing path.

The following depicts the Golden ticket, which is part of each block, albeit a solution may not be found every block:

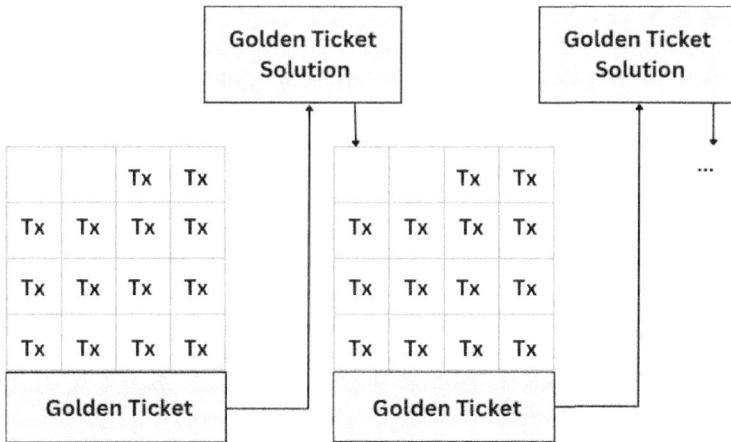

The reason why the golden ticket is so important is that it separates mining from block production as mining is not for block production, it's just to unlock the funds which provides security, and this makes attacking the network very costly. Let's first think about how PoW and PoS work and the attack vectors there. In essence, attacking a blockchain requires producing the longest chain which either requires 51% of mining power or 51% of the stake respectively. Once that is achieved the miners or validators have full control and power and will continually produce the longest chain giving them the opportunity to receive all the rewards.

In Saito this is not an issue because block production requires a node to collect and propagate transactions with fees. The only way to produce the longest chain is to collect transactions from honest nodes. If a node creates its own transaction with fees and fills a block to get 51% of the Routing Work, you will find this way is not profitable because that node then also must spend electricity power finding a hash solution for the golden ticket puzzle to get the full reward, which results in a net loss. As an extra point, the loss is not just from the attacker but other nodes that could have or should have received rewards in the process for their contribution. There is explained in more detail on this in the "Saito Security and Prevention from 51% attacks" section.

Automatic Transaction Rebroadcasting

ATR solves the Tragedy of the Commons problem by forcing old transactions to compete with new ones for space on the blockchain, thus allowing the chain to remain a reasonable size without getting bloated.

Essentially, nodes in Saito can remove the oldest blocks in the chain at certain intervals (called "Epochs") to reduce blockchain creep. Any UTXO (unspent transaction outputs) from a transaction set that contains enough tokens to pay a re-broadcasting fee must be again included in the next block. Block producers do this by creating ATR transactions (that have the original transaction data) with the newly spendable UTXO. This makes it much harder for the blockchain to grow too large and collapse.

As the blockchain expands, market competition increases the fees as there is less space for new transactions, which in turn pushes up the fees for the older transactions, helping to keep the chain pruned! There becomes a point where old data is pruned at the same rate as new data is added. This means that if old data is to remain on the chain, a fee must be paid. This prevents nodes from adding transactions to the chain that don't pay enough fees to cover the operating cost of the blockchain.

Proof of Routing Work and Architecture

The following depicts the high-level network architecture:

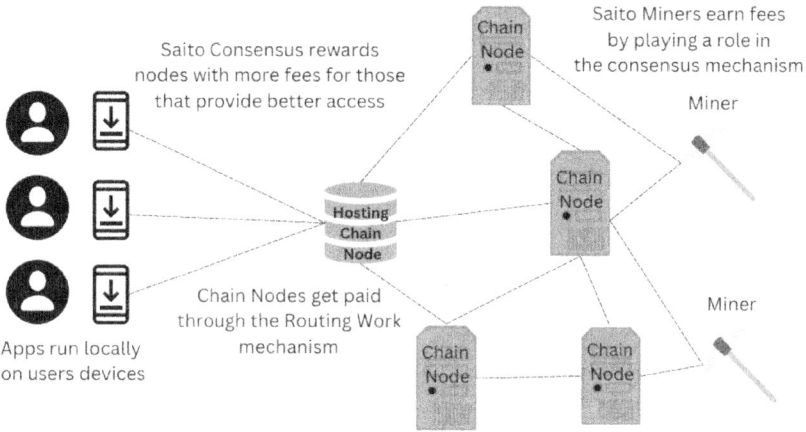

The Routing Nodes get paid for collecting fees and the Mining Nodes are paid for running the lottery in the form of the Golden Ticket system that prevents costly attacks. There are also Stakers that can stake Saito where any previous unpaid rewards are paid out to Stakers, for example, when a Golden Ticket solution is not found. However, note that this is a different mechanism to Staking in other blockchain as no actual staking service or node is required nor are delegates. Rather, it requires the user to format a special UTXO for staking. These are then added to a list of pending stakes to be included in a block.

The following diagram shows the Routing Work mechanism. This is a simplistic view showcasing a single transaction. Of course, there will be many transactions collected and broadcast by a node.

Transaction 1
Fee: 10 SAITO

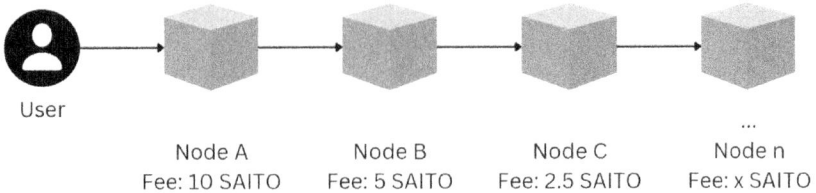

User

Node A
Fee: 10 SAITO

Node B
Fee: 5 SAITO

Node C
Fee: 2.5 SAITO

...
Node n
Fee: x SAITO

- Here, an app is running on a user's device, where a transaction is initiated.
- Nodes that are closest to the user in the transactions path to the block are paid more.
- So, Node A collects a transaction that has a fee of 10 Saito, and therefore, for simplicity has 10 Routing Work points.
- Node A then broadcasts this transaction to other nodes, in this case Node B.
- Node B collects this transaction and gets half the fee, which is 5 Saito, so 5 Routing Work points.
- Node B broadcasts this transaction to other nodes.
- Node C, upon receiving the transaction gets half the fee and Routing Work points that B got, in this case, 2.5 Saito.
- This continues until all broadcasts have finished.
- The next transaction gets accepted by a node and the process repeats.
- On this occasion it may be another node such as Node C that receives the fee closest to a user, so it gets paid more.
- Once a node has a sufficient Routing Work score that meets the "Routing Work difficulty level" it gets to produce a block.
- The Node with the highest number of Routing Work points then gets the highest chance of receiving the 50% payout of fees, dictated by the Payment Lottery.

Upon all Routing Work steps completed, and the block is produced, nobody is paid yet. The fees are all burned, and the Payment Lottery begins to decide the payout, which is 50% to a Routing Node and 50% to the Mining Node that solved the Golden Ticket.

Saito Security and prevention from 51% attacks

In Saito, the incentive structure is such that if you collect transactions from honest nodes, then those nodes are getting the best out of the network and the whole network benefits. However, what if you now try to take advantage and fill blocks with your own transactions to get 51% of routing work?

There are 2 possible situations:

- The node uses its own money to produce a block by filling up that block with all your own transactions with your own fees. That node then mines on that block to find the golden ticket and receive all the fees. The reward is divided 50-50 between the miner (that solved the golden ticket) and the block producer (that has the highest amount of Routing Work), which is yourself. This node receives all the fees in the block but there is a cost. That cost is the electricity that was spent hashing to solve the golden ticket. However, all the fees in the block were your fees! So now there is a net loss because of the electricity cost.
- The node spends its own money to produce the block, but the block's golden ticket is found by a different node. The problem here is that the node put in all the fees, but it only gets 50% of the fees back! Therefore, it's an even larger loss than the first situation.

If one now factors in that there is only a golden ticket every two blocks, essentially the loss is twice as much!

Saito is designed in such a way that a node can never receive more money than was spent, and the only profitable way is to act as an honest node by using other normal users' transaction fees. That way it's not an issue because any money spent on hash power is paid off by the rewards from the block.

Saito and the Free market

It is often thought that the free market can decide how the network is paid for in the case of PoS and PoW. However, it has been proven time and time again over the course of history that this leads to Monopolization, Cartelization and Privatization. The issue is that the private sector creates a barrier to data sharing to maximize profit, Infura in the context of Ethereum being a prime example.

Essentially, the Saito Team claims that the following is happening:

- In most blockchains that are scalable, Miners and Stakers do not want to pay the cost of running their own nodes, but rather delegating that responsibility to others, such as is the case with the Ethereum network where everybody is free riding on Infura.
- All the rewards and control are centralized to the Miners and Stakers respectively, creating a monopoly dominated by mining and staking pools because it's only Miners and Stakers that get paid. Some may debate that this is not the case, but it potentially could be unless there is a better incentive mechanism that allows the network to pay for itself.

Therefore, it's clear that trying to let the free market decide is creating a potential problem of monopolization.

Saito's approach to Openness, not just Decentralization

The Saito team claims that many blockchains advertise themselves as decentralized or certainly, that's the goal. However, due to what has been explained in previous sections in this chapter this could be seen as nothing more than a buzzword. What is more important is the concept of openness. Many blockchains are not as open as they should be, in that not anyone can join. This is important because openness yields decentralization.

If we take Bitcoin as an example, the huge innovation was that it was open in that anyone could join, at least at first, but this is now becoming less the case.

Ethereum also has largely created a barrier with the minimum stake of 32 ETH to become a validator. Those that want to run a node that isn't a mining or staking node have little financial incentive.

Bitcoin's second innovation was that it was self-sufficient, in that honest nodes were incentivized to secure the network and deter attackers, and this created a trustless network. The key here is that openness and self-sufficiency created a trustless network.

However, even if blockchain networks are decentralized does that necessarily make it open? Can anyone simply join? This is an open question for you to ponder. The Saito Team have created this thought experiment to help with this question:

If the network is open but not self-sufficient (because it cannot pay for itself), it will result in that network being run by a large monopoly like Amazon.

If it can pay for itself, but it's not open, then essentially you have created the banking system.

Openness is not free; the network needs to support it. Initially volunteers supported and paid for blockchain networks but as they scaled more, the volunteer provision shifted to profiting companies in the private sector, think Infura for Ethereum.

Therefore, Saito's solution using its consensus mechanism of Proof of Routing Work, creates free competition and incentives using the collection and sharing of fees to support and pay for the network. This makes the network open and self-sufficient with no chance of either of these two properties breaking down.

Tokenomics

The maximum token supply is 8,000,000,000 tokens which will enter circulation over the next 20 years. There are currently 3,000,000,000 tokens in circulation, primarily in the form of ERC20 or BEP20 tokens. These can be migrated to the native token via a bridge which is part of the "Dawn of Persistence" phase in their roadmap.

The tokens are used for transaction fees in the network and paying rewards to Routing Nodes, Mining Nodes and Staking Nodes.

Also, the tokenomics has been designed such that users can decide which applications and servers deserve financing by the Saito network in that those that attract high usage are subsidized by the consensus mechanism indirectly.

The distribution is:

- 33.3% in public circulation (at the time of writing)
- 8.3% to Core team
- 11.1% to funding development
- 47.2% for network incentives

The tokenomics, at the time of writing, is still a work in progress as the roadmap is rolled out.

Final thoughts

The interesting angle here is although Saito removes the 51% attack issue or any trend towards centralized control (through its Proof of Routing Work consensus and openness and self-sufficiency properties), is it just solving a real problem or a theoretical problem? For example, thus far Bitcoin and Ethereum have not suffered a 51% attack (although other blockchains with a lower hash rate have), but that doesn't mean it's still not possible in future. At least Saito may offer that peace of mind. The question really becomes, will the market or the masses catch on to this? In the end, to gain real adoption new users need to come onboard or move from other existing blockchains. For that to happen, those new users need to perceive a 51% attack or large centralized control as a realistic threat to warrant them moving across. Once a strong network effect is in place many users tend to remain on a given platform and new users tend to be onboarded to that same platform, even if there is a better platform alternative. It needs to be significantly better for users to switch. There are countless examples of this in the technology space. This is an open point for you to think about!

For Saito though, it's not the 51% attack threat that is the largest issue here, but rather the solving of the Trilemma, essentially by removing the Trilemma! So, by removing the Trilemma the rest "comes out in the wash", meaning that the 51% attack is removed automatically because of its security mechanism, openness and self-sufficiency, simply rendering a 51% attack completely pointless. You now have a system that is open, self-sufficient, decentralized, scalable and secure.

It's a genius solution that simply remains to be seen if it catches on or whether other blockchains are "good enough" and since they already have the power of the network effect, this may just continue. Many in the community have a view that a blockchain doesn't need to be decentralized fully as long as it's "good enough". "Good enough" meaning that if its secure and scalable but not fully decentralized, this may be sufficient. If Ethereum can scale in the end, perhaps the perceived centralization aspect isn't a huge issue, or is it? Do we want to wait until it becomes an issue? Or like Saito, do we want to be proactive, thus removing any potential concerns?

References

The following references contain more detail from a technical and ecosystem perspective to expand your knowledge:

Saito whitepaper:

https://saito.io/saito-whitepaper.pdf

Main Saito portal with website, whitepaper and technology breakdown:

https://saito.io

A reference to selfish mining is here:

https://www.investopedia.com/terms/s/selfish-mining.asp

Bittensor

Brief History

Bittensor was created by software developers Jacob Robert Steeves and Ala Shabaana and launched in 2021 by the Opentensor Foundation as a decentralized AI platform. The vision was to build a peer-to-peer neural network where those peers can build, train and share Machine Learning (ML) models in a decentralized, transparent, open source and more collaborative manner in contrast to the current centralized AI model which is highly controlled and censored.

It utilizes the Polkadot substrate framework and initially had a Polkadot Parachain slot reserved. However, after this, the Finney Fork was a strategic move to allow Bittensor to become its own blockchain separate from the Polkadot parachain system, although still using the substrate framework.

It is key to understand that essentially Bittensor is a neural network, is a computational model that processes information in a similar way to biological neural networks of animal brains. Therefore, it's designed to facilitate the exchange of Machine Learning (ML) models through peers in the network to allow a collective intelligence to form a digital hive mind.

Bittensor also creates a marketplace for AI and therefore transforms machine intelligence into a tradable commodity resulting in lots of innovation from the global community.

The utility token for this market is called TAO which has a limited supply of 21,000,000 tokens and follows a similar tokenomic model to Bitcoin. The only way TAO comes into existence is through mining, where currently about 6,500,000 TAO has been mined. In addition to miners mining TAO, there are also validators to maintain the integrity, quality of data and models being exchanged.

The overall vision is to leverage the most advancing technology today, being Artificial Intelligence, in a such a way to benefit the community where it is also controlled by the community.

What Problem is Bittensor Trying to Solve?

Bittensor was created to address many specific problems in the realm of AI, particularly the centralization of AI and monopolistic control of the AI technologies themselves. The current issue is that large corporations don't share the AI code and algorithms because it's not open source and in addition to this any new knowledge learned by a node is only shared within its own ecosystem. Essentially, this creates an opaque system of AI where these corporations maximize their own interests for profit. For example, OpenAI's code (for chatGPT) is not open source, and it's widely lauded that the answers provided are what it wants to tell you rather than what it needs to tell you. This is all due to centralized control, but what if this system could be decentralized with economic incentives for the users? What if developers could enhance the source code more freely in an open and shared manner? This would create a shared approach to AI where in a holistic sense, machine learning models and AI in general becomes stronger overall. Knowledge is power, but shared knowledge is even more powerful. From an analogous angle, the reason why YouTube became so successful is down to the sharing of knowledge in a decentralized manner, which benefits everyone. However, a fully decentralized version of this could be even more powerful because YouTube is still a centralized entity with censorship and control, even though any user can create their own channel. This is diverging from the context of AI but is just an example why sharing knowledge and decentralization is powerful.

Bittensor sought to break down these walls with approaching AI in a decentralized manner by creating a network of "neurons" allowing a vast range of entities to benefit from machine learning. This provides a more inclusive and democratic approach by allowing users to contribute their computational resources to drive innovation and with a more ethical stance, where users can be given answers to questions without bias or manipulation. This creates a peer-to-peer model and marketplace where different AI models are connected using an incentive mechanism via the Bittensor blockchain to provide an auditable trail of knowledge and learning activities.

The incentive mechanism works by producing a market where intelligence is paid for by other intelligence systems in a peer-to-peer fashion across the network. The peers rank each other by training others within the network and there is a score based on the performance of those nodes from the knowledge they accumulated. The score is tracked on the blockchain ledger, and the highest ranked peers receive a monetary reward in TAO.

From an economic perspective Bittensor miners and validators are rewarded with TAO tokens using a tokenomic model very similar to Bitcoin to provide scarcity with no pre mine of TAO tokens. The only way TAO tokens come into the system is from mining them, just like Bitcoin, although the mechanism of mining is different in Bittensor.

Nodes in Bittensor share data and resources to train AI models effectively. They do not directly share the models themselves but instead the outcomes produced by these models. If a mining node is tasked with a prediction algorithm, it doesn't directly share the model or algorithm. Rather, it contributes to the overall collective intelligence of the network by providing predictions. Validators then assess these prediction outputs for quality and accuracy. Nodes then adjust their models over time based on feedback from the network, and as a result the intelligence of the network improves. This is an indirect method of knowledge sharing which results in more efficient and accurate machine learning models while keeping the privacy of each node's data intact. This leads into the next section on Neural Networks.

Neural Networks

To understand Bittensor as a network a little more, let's first grasp the concept of Neural Networks. As briefly described earlier, it's like the biological neural networks of animal brains.

A neural network consists of layers of interconnected nodes called **neurons** that each carry out a single computation. An input layer receives the data and at least one hidden layer processes that data and an output layer then produces the result.

Each neuron takes the input from other neurons where if the total combined input is greater than a particular threshold the output gets passed to the next layer. There is a weight determined by the strength of these connections between the neurons and this dictates how much one neuron influences another.

The network receives feedback during training and learns by adjusting these weights accordingly. Essentially during this training, the purpose of the adjustment of these weights is to minimize the difference between the predictions of the networks and its outcomes.

Neural networks can then carry out tasks such as prediction modelling, games and speech recognition, allowing them to be a powerful tool for computers to learn and make predictions and decisions accordingly.

To piece this all together it's important to understand the difference between an AI Algorithm and an AI Model.

An **AI Algorithm** is a set of rules or followed to perform a task. They are used to process data and make decisions. They are essentially recipes to instruct the system how to learn from data and make predictions. Examples include Decision Trees and in the case of Bittensor, Neural Networks.

An **AI Model** is the output result of an AI algorithm applied to data. It's the learned component that makes predictions or decisions. It's the "brain" that's been trained and molded by the algorithm using the input data. The model is deployed to carry out tasks like image recognition for example.

In summary, the AI Algorithm is the method, and the AI Model is the product of applying that method to data. The quality of an AI model depends on both the algorithm used and the data it was trained on.

The following illustrates a neural network in action with the different layers where upon learning the result is the ability to identify an image:

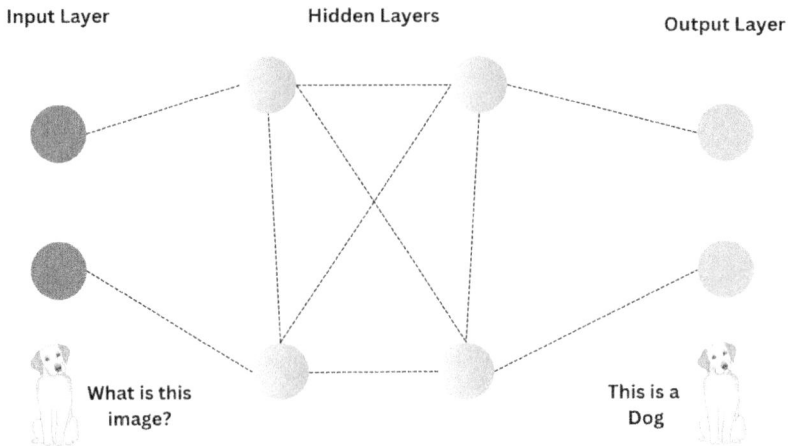

Input Layer   Hidden Layers   Output Layer

What is this image?   This is a Dog

The image of the dog is the result produced by the AI model. Therefore, there is a prediction that the image is a dog after the conclusion of the AI model after analyzing all the data through all the layers. The model has been trained with many images and has learned to recognize patterns to characterize a dog and when it sees a new image it uses the learned knowledge to determine if the image is a dog or not. Therefore, the output is the result of the AI model's processing and learning, which is applied to the input data (the image) to generate a prediction (thus concluding it to be a dog).

Proof of Useful Work vs Proof of Work

Bittensor's consensus mechanism (Proof of Intelligence) is explained in more detail in the section on "Bittensor Consensus Mechanism". However, Proof of Intelligence (PoI) in summary, is a form of Proof of Work that differs from that used by Bitcoin for example. In PoW, miners solve complex mathematical puzzles which do nothing useful directly. The use is in securing the network, but a mathematical puzzle solution as output otherwise is not useful at all. What if, as well as securing the network, there could be a more useful piece of work done that benefits the network and community as a whole? This is where PoI is used where it leverages computational resources, not to just solve a maths puzzle but rather to train AI models, in the form of Machine Learning, improving AI overall. The whole ecosystem becomes stronger from an AI perspective as nodes continually train and learn, which can be seen as a form of **Proof of Useful Work (PoUW)**.

In the PoI model (a form of PoUW), the miners are rewarded based on the performance and quality of the AI models generated. This helps to advance AI and has a more tangible benefit than just maths puzzles solved in traditional PoW.

So essentially, PoI in Bittensor yields a more productive use of power and energy while aligning with the interest of not just securing the network, but at the same time contributing to advancements in AI. This grows AI, thus making AI stronger and all this knowledge is shared collectively by nodes in the network. The important thing to understand is this is on a global, open level rather than confined within a particular entity such as a corporation that does not share the AI models outside of that centralized entity.

Bittensor Consensus Mechanism

Bittensor is rather unique compared to other blockchains as there are two facets to its consensus mechanism, one for incentives and dividends for miners and validators respectively and one for block creation and validation of transactions.

It uses **Yuma Consensus** to reward miners (in incentives) based on their performance and rewards validators (in dividends) for their assessment of the miner's performance.

Proof of Authority (PoA) is used for creating and validating blocks where these nodes are hosted by the OpenTensor Foundation.

In summary, Yuma Consensus utilizes elements of PoW and PoS which in combination, in the context of Bittensor, is Proof of Intelligence. Also, PoA is the consensus mechanism for block creation and validation, and these mechanisms all work together.

Yuma Consensus

Yuma Consensus is a stake-weighted approach to reward miners based on their performance for the tasks they are given and rewards validators for their evaluations of that performance in agreement with other validators to ensure fair distribution of those rewards. Essentially, it's a hybrid consensus mechanism where elements of PoW and PoS are used where nodes perform computational work, and the performance is verified by other nodes. The work, as mentioned earlier in this chapter, is machine learning and nodes are rewarded for their performance, hence the name Proof of Intelligence (PoI). Miners are the producers of knowledge and validators are the extractors of the knowledge produced.

As a precursor to this, there are many subnets running on Bittensor (discussed in a later section in this chapter) and tasks involving computational work will vary depending on the subnet. For example, the task could be related to providing storage space, machine translation, predictions or responding to a text prompt. This all depends on the subnet as a subnet in Bittensor is dedicated to a specific role. All these subnets are connected to the single blockchain, which in Bittensor is known as **subtensor**.

A step-by-step summary of Yuma Consensus is as follows. Think of the miners and validators as working within a subnet, hence subnet miners and subnet validators:

- Miners carry out tasks given by validators involving computational work related to machine learning tasks and submit this to the network.
- Validators then assess the miners' work based on performance. They evaluate the solutions based on certain aspects such as intelligence, speed and diversity.
- Validators then express their view about the performance of the miners through a set of weights and these are aggregated across all validators to produce a weight matrix. This is the basis for a set of rankings set by validators.
- The weight matrix influences consensus and incentives by translating it into incentives for miners and dividends for validators.

- Miners receive incentive rewards from validators based on the quality of their work.
- Validators producing evaluations that align with consensus are rewarded with dividends based on the amount of stake they hold.
- There are also nominators that receive rewards (these are those that delegate their stake to validators).

So, there are two scores, being a **dividends score** that validators receive based on how well they evaluate the performance of miners and an **incentive score** that miners receive based on the tasks they perform and the quality of their work.

Every 12 seconds a new TAO is minted which is split across 32 subnets meaning that a given subnet gets a fraction of this TAO based on its performance. The distribution within a subnet is such that 18% goes to the subnet owner, 41% to the subnet validators (the dividend) and 41% to the subnet miners (the incentive). Note that the distribution of rewards is not specifically every 12 seconds but rather after about 100-200 blocks (as this is when validators send the updated ranking weights to the blockchain). At the rate of 1 TAO every 12 seconds that equates to 7200 TAO created each day.

Another key point is if a validator misbehaves, it can be penalized. For example, let's say a validator chooses a miner that subjectively thinks has performed well in contrast to another 100 validators. It's then proven that its cherry-picked certain miners and has a degree of bias which is not allowed in Yuma Consensus.

One may ask what model or approach determines the calculation of rewards? Is it proprietary to Bittensor? The answer is not exactly. Bittensor has not reinvented the wheel as such. There is an existing concept in cooperative game theory called the **Shapley Value** where it's currently used to allocate rewards in multi-player settings. To be clear, the term "multi-player settings" is a broad concept that applies to any scenario where multiple participants (or players) are involved and contribute to a common goal or outcome. This can be in gaming, AI models or anything similar. This then can be used to fit the environment of a decentralized AI network. The concept is used to distribute rewards fairly to participants where those users have contributed to an overall outcome.

Let's visualize a game in Bittensor where each model contributes to the network. The Shapley Value is a calculation that computes the value of each participant by imagining what the network could lose if that participant was not present. Essentially, it measures the impact of each contribution to the success of the network. In the context of Bittensor, this value is then translated in Yuma Consensus to determine the value contributed to the network and thus corresponding reward distributions, ensuring that rewards are proportional to the value added. This in turn, encourages participants to perform better and continuously improve their work and models.

The following depicts the interaction between an end user, validator and miner in Yuma Consensus:

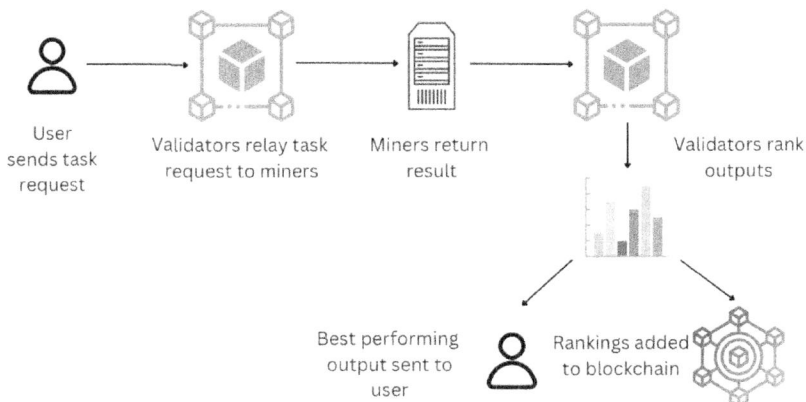

User sends task request

Validators relay task request to miners

Miners return result

Validators rank outputs

Best performing output sent to user

Rankings added to blockchain

In Bittensor, the word mining and validation are not related to traditional Bitcoin mining or validation of blocks. Bittensor mining is subnet mining and validation is subnet validation as per the tasks completed and competition in Yuma Consensus. The creation and validation of blocks is where PoA comes in as we will see next.

Proof of Authority (PoA)

PoA is used in the context of Bittensor for block creation and validation. Let's first explore how standard PoA works in general:

- Validators are selected based on trustworthiness or authority status. There is a vetting process for validators to ensure they meet certain standards. As a part of this process, the validators will need to have their identities formally approved by the network.
- The process of ID verification is a combination of human oversight and automation where identification data is cross-checked with public databases.
- Potential validators stake tokens against their reputation.
- Validators produce blocks and confirm transactions in a rotation approach.
- A limited set of pre-approved validators validate these transactions.
- Consensus is reached typically through a voting process via the pre-approved validators.

PoA is often used for private or consortium blockchains where trust among validators is established. Note that it's more energy efficient than PoW but less decentralized than PoS in general.

In the context of Bittensor, there are some unique characteristics it has as part of its PoA mechanism. Firstly, the blockchain, known as subtensor records all key information of the connected subnets where the subnets are different markets within the overall network. Secondly, although Bittensor is not a private blockchain, the Authority Nodes are hosted by the Opentensor Foundation which is an organization being the driving force behind the Bittensor network. Thirdly, the focus of the reward structure mainly stems from Yuma Consensus and not from the PoA mechanism itself.

Bittensor Network Architecture

The Bittensor network contains 3 main components:

A competition based on incentives: As per the decentralized nature of Bittensor, one can create their own incentive mechanism or participate in an existing competition. Each competition with incentives is known as a subnet. An example could be price predictions for an asset where the miner that gives the best prediction receives an incentive reward in TAO. Another example is text prompting where a validator sends a prompt, and a miner produces a prompt completion. The best performing miners on this text prompting subnet are rewarded.

The blockchain (subtensor): This runs the subnets and ensures that the competitive market adheres to fundamental principles such as being permissionless, decentralized and resistant to manipulation to avoid validators or miners colluding. For example, miners could collude and group together to produce answers that are not unique to receive rewards. Validators could also choose their "favourite" miners to reward, conflicting with the agreement of many other validators. Such an action would result in punishment for that validator.

Bittensor API: This connects all the subnets and the blockchain itself. An API stands for Application Programming Interface. Essentially it contains all the main functions, for example subnet validators to interact with the blockchain via an interface. The validator issues a request for a task, and this is called via a function in the API which then submits this to the blockchain. The blockchain then calls another function in the API to distribute rewards to validators and miners as per the tasks carried out.

The following illustrates the interaction of subnet miners, subnet validators, the incentive mechanism and the blockchain via the Bittensor API in Yuma Consensus:

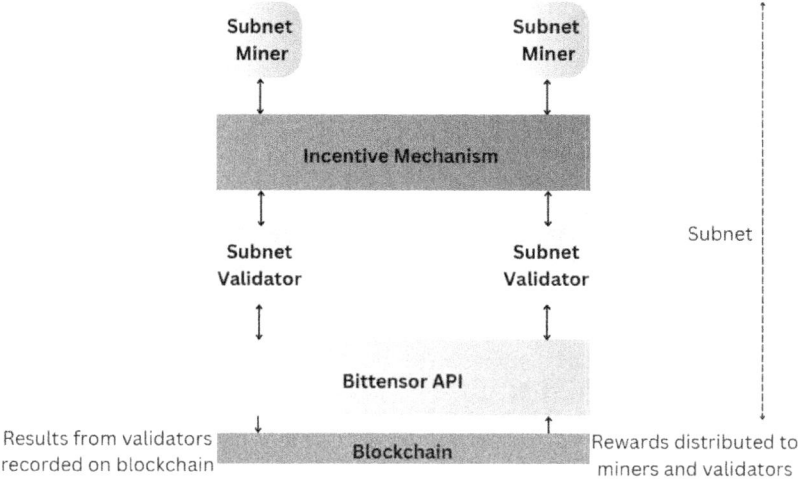

It should be noted that tasks themselves run at the API layer, not on the blockchain, but the results are recorded on the blockchain.

Subnets

A subnet is a competitive market where any user can create a subnet or partake in an existing subnet. There is a registration cost in TAO and upon registration a subnet netuid is allocated to the user. The participation is in the form of a subnet miner or subnet validator where the user requires enough computing resources, a registration and a wallet.

Once the miner or validator is set up the competition works by validators allocating miners tasks where all miners are given the same task. The miner responds with the results upon which a ranking of the work done occurs by the validators to assess the quality of the task carried out. The validators are also rewarded as they ensure that the highest quality miners are rewarded with their work based on performance which helps to improve the overall quality of that subnet to maintain continuous improvement of the models and tasks. In summary, the incentive mechanism is unique to the subnet.

As a high-level summary the steps shown earlier in Yuma Consensus can now be shown in the context of subnets:

- Subnet miners perform some useful work in the context of that subnet given by a validator.
- The subnet validators assess the tasks completed by the subnet miners.
- The subnet validators all come to an agreement with their opinion on the work produced by the miners.
- All these opinions are input to the Yuma Consensus via the Bittensor API and recorded on the blockchain.
- In each subnet there could be more than one miner rewarded for their work and this is weighted based on performance. Likewise, validator rewards are weighted by their stake of TAO tokens. This is all part of Yuma Consensus.

The rewards are not distributed in every 12 second block but rather at a much larger interval to ensure consistent performance as also the updated rankings sent by the validators are at a larger interval of many blocks to allow time for collection and calculation of performance data. The rewards are distributed to the best performing miners and validators for every subnet (in this case there are currently 32 subnets).

Mixture of Experts (MoE)

In the centralized world specific AI models can be very siloed where a task required for running code to translate English to French using just one model may produce average results. However, if there are separate models where model is for programming and the other is for language translation this will yield better results. This approach allows experts to collaborate with each other thus exceeding the capabilities of a single expert. This also means more accurate predictions and the ability to process larger volumes of data which enables the network to give more precise answers with respect to a single model as per the centralized systems. An example of this is exemplified with applications running on Bittensor such as Nous Finetuning, where different subnets can interact via inter-subnet bridging where a subnet geared for a particular application can collaborate with another subnet geared for a different application to maximize the overall result. Nous Finetuning is described later in this chapter.

What is the relevance of the AI tasks set by validators?

Typically, Bittensor is seen as a Proof of Useful Work chain in the form of PoI, which leads many to think that mathematical puzzles are solved as per the traditional approach in Bitcoin for example. Although this may be partly the case, the bulk of the work is tasks that are relevant to the subnet being prompting, predictions and language translation to name a few. For example, there are 32 subnets where subnet 2 is used for machine translation, subnet 5 for image generation and subnet 32 for 3D generation.

Applications running and building on Bittensor

Subnets are essentially a platform to allow applications to be built and run where end users interact with these applications for the relevant subnet.

The question is what is the incentive for users or corporations to build and run on Bittensor? The answer is in addition to incentives and rewards as already mentioned in this chapter, corporations could dramatically reduce their costs. Data warehouses are a huge overhead for many AI corporations as well as hosting the infrastructure itself. Imagine if this could all be outsourced to the Bittensor network? There would be much less requirement to host the infrastructure as this is already hosted by Bittensor being the subnets, the validators and miners. This is especially advantageous for small startups who don't want to bear the cost of capital for equipment and therefore is a huge saving for them. Other incentives revolve around governance where stakeholders can have a say in the future of the ecosystem in terms of the network's operation and development.

There are many applications now running on Bittensor across the 32 subnets. AIT was officially the first to register a subnet. The following lists a few applications to demonstrate the potential for Bittensor to become a thriving ecosystem for AI.

AIT

AIT Protocol is a Bittensor Neural Network developing a marketplace for ML specifically in Mathematics, Logical Reasoning and Data Analytics. The goal for AIT is to provide a subnet tailored for computation of mathematical operations and analytics, helping Bittensor to enhance its ecosystem. The aim is to enable enterprises and startup companies to use these advanced resources via APIs for real world use cases. In turn, this integration will render opportunities for the community to set up miners and earn AIT tokens related to training of models.

TensorSpace

This is an AI platform to allow democratization for the deployment of AI applications where an interface enables users to build and tune GPT models without requiring any code or deep knowledge. Typically, complex processes are needed for AI model development, but this approach with TensorSpace simplifies it for AI and ML developers and researchers. The integration with Bittensor leverages a decentralized marketplace for users to borrow and lend resources like TPUs and GPUs which are essential for AI tasks and training neural networks.

Nous

Nous Finetuning is a team stemming from Nous Research who are focused on Large Scale Language Model architecture and data synthesis. The fine-tuning application is dedicated to fine tuning large language models and runs on

Subnet 6, and it interacts with Subnet 18 where extra fine tuning occurs. The Nous subnet rewards miners for fine tuning LLMs with data from subnet 18 and is therefore the first subnet to perform cross boundary communication with another subnet.

Architecture for Applications utilizing the Bittensor Ecosystem

The following depicts the Bittensor architecture with applications running on the platform:

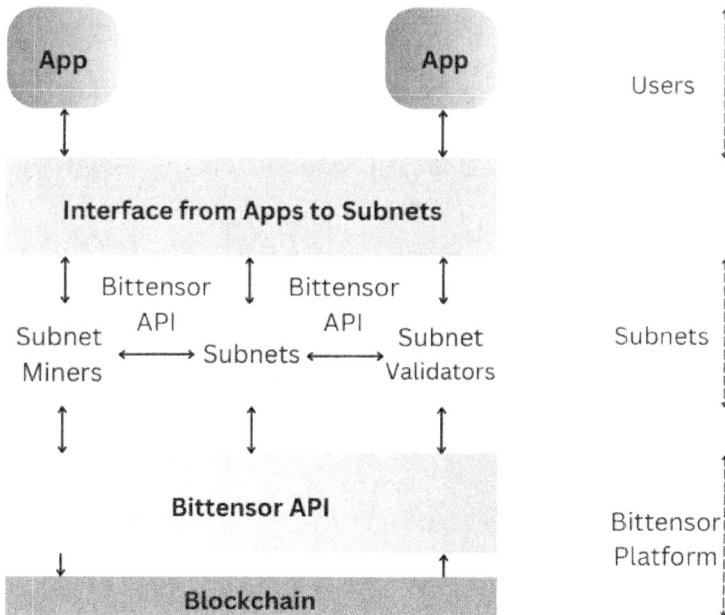

Bittensor vs other AI platforms

This table summarizes some key differences between Bittensor and other AI platforms (like AGIX or Ocean). Note, this doesn't necessarily mean Bittensor as a platform is better or worse, but rather to highlight that other ecosystems are different for different purposes. Some for example as used as a marketplace for AI products and services. Bittensor is a purely Layer 1 blockchain, in essence like Bitcoin but leveraging AI. Many blockchain AI solutions run on existing chains like Ethereum or Solana and are application specific. Bittensor has its own dedicated blockchain and any AI application can run on Bittensor via subnets making it a general-purpose AI blockchain.

	Bittensor	Other AI platforms
Tokenomics	Similar to Bitcoin and limited supply of 21 million. Only created by mining.	Maybe limited in supply, but the tokens don't only exist by mining them, some are pre mined.
Consensus mechanism	Proof of Intelligence under Yuma Consensus and Proof of Authority for block creation and validation.	Most are Proof of Stake or Proof of Authority. In the case of Render it uses specific consensus called Proof of Render.
Layer 1 or Layer 2 chain	Layer 1 blockchain.	Many run as Layer 2 on other Layer 1 blockchains to offer flexibility.
General Purpose AI or Application Specific	General Purpose, AI applications run on relevant subnets	Some are platforms but many are application specific such as GPU rendering, 3D rendering or gaming.

Tokenomics

The tokenomics follow a similar vein to Bitcoin which of course has seen huge success. The limit is 21 million TAO and the only way for TAO to exist is through the mining process. There was no IPO or pre mine of tokens.

The issuance schedule of TAO still results in halving every 4 years like Bitcoin. However, the schedule is such that 1 TAO is emitted every 12 second block. Once half of the supply has been issued the rate of issuance is then halved and this equates to halving every 4 years. This continues until all 21 million TAO are in circulation and results in TAO being disinflationary because the amount of inflation is steadily decreasing.

TAO token utility

As already mentioned, TAO is used for rewards distribution to miners and validators. For participants to receive rewards they need to stake TAO. This form of collateral helps to ensure participants act in the best interests of the network. It can also be used for delegated staking where token holders stake their TAO to earn APY after selecting a validator. At the time of writing about 90% of TAO is staked! This is very bullish for price because any TAO staked is essentially not part of the circulating supply, contributing to its scarcity even further.

In addition to staking, TAO is also used for governance where users can vote on future proposals in the network. It is also used as payment for accessing AI services and applications built on Bittensor and fees are also paid in TAO for when transactions occur.

Final Thoughts

Overall, Yuma Consensus appears to be a real game changer for Bittensor and has a high degree of inclusivity from the perspective of calculating the rewards of each subnet but also the reward allocation ratio of each subnet miner and subnet validator within a subnet. What is also impressive is that many contributions are factored into the performance of a task given to a miner such as human contribution, big data, computational power and intelligence. This all allows applications running on subnets to improve the value of the network and relish in the incentives.

Some possible issues with Yuma Consensus revolve around the limit in the number of subnets accommodated by Bittensor. Currently 32 subnets likely are not enough to compete with the centralized AI world. However, Bittensor has plans to increase the number of subnets to 1024 which allows more teams to join the network thus fiercely increasing competition among different subnets. An extra component to factor in is the competition among subnets where a given subnet must consistently perform to receive rewards. For example, in theory, if a subnet has low performance, it may be replaced by a new subnet. However, some subnets have duplicated resources and have many common themes such as text to image and text prompts which could lead to a reduction in competition of subnets. Once again, the Opentensor Foundation are resolving this.

The general-purpose approach of Bittensor has been attractive right from the start where many different AI applications can simply be subnets on Bittensor and with their own tokens such as AIT Protocol. Any enterprise or startup company can build and run on the network, cutting their costs when compared to the centralized model. With the extra flavors of open source, collaboration, rewards, a strong tokenomics model and the thirst to constantly improve the strength of AI, it's likely Bittensor will become a major rival to centralized AI giants.

References

The following links provide more detail on the Bittensor ecosystem:

Official site with information on consensus mechanism:

https://bittensor.com/

Bittensor whitepaper:

https://bittensor.com/whitepaper

High level Introduction to Bittensor:

https://docs.bittensor.com/learn/introduction

Yuma Consensus:

https://docs.bittensor.com/yuma-consensus

Details on Shapley Value, Bittensor Consensus and Network Architecture:

https://bittensor.org/

Bittensor FAQ:

https://docs.bittensor.com/questions-and-answers

Description of Proof of Authority:

https://www.coindesk.com/learn/what-is-proof-of-authority/

Comparison of Different Blockchains by Performance and Adoption

This section shows a comparison between different blockchains by transactions per second (tps) and finality. It also shows bar charts for current daily transactions, daily active users and current transactions per second. For purpose of comparison, it shows a few other blockchain platforms not covered in this book. For some of the tables and bar charts, a few blockchains in this book have been omitted mainly because it's very early in the adoption phase and there is a lack of information on these. For extra comparison however, other blockchains not covered in this book have been included.

It should be clarified that this is an evolving landscape and the figures in this chapter can get out of date fairly quickly. However, as more information arises the numbers can be revised and updated in future editions.

A mention on transactions per second (tps)

The measure of transactions per second can be represented differently by different blockchains and this poses a challenge when attempting to compare them side by side. This is compounded by the fact that transactions are formatted differently for different blockchains and the transactions themselves take different forms (such as simple payments, smart contract executions or batched transactions). Therefore, it's important to understand that not all transactions are equal.

There are other ways to measure the performance of a blockchain and these include:

- **UOPS (User Ops per Second)**: UOPS considers the computational value of each operation and is therefore the number of user operations processed per second, when taking into account transaction complexity.
- **Latency**: This is the time taken for a transaction to be confirmed or processed, where the lower the latency the faster.
- **Finality**: The time taken for an irreversible confirmation of a transaction or block, meaning that once confirmed, it cannot be altered. To clarify, block time is not the same as finality. For example,

Bitcoin has 10-minute blocks, but this doesn't mean the transaction is completely irreversible after 10 minutes. Bitcoin requires six confirmations and therefore, its finality is 60 minutes. To emphasize, the finality for Bitcoin is probabilistic finality because even after six confirmations it's possible a transaction could be reversed, but the chance is astronomically low.

As a user of a blockchain, they don't care too much about tps, but rather more so on latency and finality. This is because a user of a blockchain wants their transaction to be processed with little delay and confirmed as quickly as possible. This is an argument as to why finality is often a better measure than tps because one main principle of blockchain technology is that of immutability. Despite this, for the purpose of ease of comparison in this book, tps and finality are used rather than other measures because there is more information publicly available on these.

However, on the topic of inequality in transactions, one example of a blockchain that measures tps differently is Solana and hence its tps figures are somewhat inflated. This is because Solana's tps includes user transactions and consensus votes where about 85% of the tps number arises from these votes. However, it's clear that Solana is still one of the fastest blockchains and even with the figures reduced to filter out the consensus votes, it's still much higher than most other chains. The figure quoted in the comparison table is the inflated (unfiltered number). This is because it aligns with most references on other websites and youtube videos and thus causes less confusion for those that cross reference these numbers.

In summary, measuring performance fairly and accurately is difficult, so as the reader you must take the figures with a "little pinch of salt" because they are subject to change and there is no complete standard for tps. However, it's the best we have at this point and these numbers are also more publicly available for comparison. Therefore, it's important to treat the tps and finality numbers as a rough guide to understand how different blockchains compare in terms of performance. Overall, the comparison tables and graphs should be of some interest for the reader to provide a "general feel" for the current performance and progress of each blockchain, albeit with some caveats.

Comparison table of tps and finality for each blockchain

The comparison table in this section mainly focuses on the performance of each blockchain with some future potential numbers upon improved scalability. It should be emphasized that performance and scalability, although often used interchangeably, do have slightly different meanings. **Performance** measures what a system is currently capable of achieving and **scalability** measures the ability of a system to improve performance by adding more resources. In the context of blockchain, scalability is the ability for the network to handle an increasing volume of transactions even as the network grows. One approach to improving scalability is implementing layer 2s or sharding and parallelization for example, thus allowing the network to handle more transactions to improve performance overall.

Now that this has been clarified, this is the definition of each value measure in the comparison table:

Current tps: This is a range of the current number of transactions per second that the blockchain is processing on mainnet at the current level of adoption.

This information is generally available in block explorers for the respective chain. Some sources (especially the official site for the respective chain) quote higher numbers than what the blockchain may be processing on a usual day (the lower range value) where this number is the upper range value (achieved under peak demand) shown in the table. It's likely that the chain can handle much more, but other measures in the table provide this.

The lower range tps number is important because this is the tps being processed under normal demand and therefore shows the usage of the platform, although quite often it can be somewhere between the lower and upper range tps. It can peak to the upper range but this is not "the norm". While this upper range number is useful to know, the lower range number gives an indication of the usage and demand. After all, if there is little demand or adoption the upper range number is less significant. However, some of these blockchains are in their

255

early stage of adoption, hence in the course of time the lower range number may consistently increase.

Max tps: This is the maximum number of transactions per second that can be processed on testnet. Essentially, it's the maximum tps that could be processed on mainnet with increased adoption (hence simulated on testnet).

This is a useful measure because it shows what the network can handle with high demand and load. It should be emphasized that this measure is generally not "the norm" on mainnet either due to lack of demand or differences between the mainnet and testnet environments. The intention is that testnets are as close as possible to mimicking mainnets. The max tps is a key number as this value should be achievable on mainnet at some point when demand is very high. However, anyone with a software development and testing background would understand that test environments (in blockchains known as testnets) and production environments (in blockchains known as mainnets) are different because of the random nature of production environments that cannot always be simulated by test environments. In summary, production systems rarely achieve theoretical capacity, especially on blockchains.

On a slightly different note, from a security perspective, hackers want to hack mainnets as that's where the funds are as opposed to testnets which are just fake funds for testing purposes.

Max Theoretical tps: This shows the number of transactions per second that is theoretically possible with extra scalability measures (but may or may not have been proven on a testnet yet). For example, full danksharding in Ethereum is a scalability implementation to improve performance. Another approach is that used by Kadena, possibly deploying up to 1000 parallel chains on mainnet in future.

Current Finality: The current finality time for the blockchain, where this is the time taken for a transaction to become irreversible once it's added to a block.

Lowest Theoretical Finality: The lowest possible finality time that has been proven on testnet or is theoretically possible but may not have been demonstrated on testnet yet.

It should be noted that some measures are not known and so have the value "Unknown". In the future these figures can be updated as more information is found.

	Current tps	Max tps	Max Theoretical tps	Current Finality	Lowest Theoretical Finality
Solana	3000 - 5000	50000	710000	2 - 12 secs	400ms
Kadena	160 - 400	1000	50000	90 secs	1.5 secs
Kaspa	2 - 400	4000	30000	10 - 13 secs	Unknown
Ethereum	10 - 30	Unknown	100000	13 - 15 mins	12 secs
Sei	30 - 50	28300	Unknown	390 - 400ms	250 ms
Algorand	10 - 30	6000	46000	0	0
Pulsechain	2 - 35	53	Unknown	13 - 15 mins	Unknown
Bitcoin	5 - 7	Unknown	Unknown	60 mins	60 mins

The following are some extra notes on each chain for the table above:

Solana

Current tps: As already mentioned, the Solana tps includes consensus votes and user transactions, thus inflating the tps number more than other chains. Once the consensus votes are filtered out, the tps is about 300 – 1000, which is still much higher than most other blockchains.

Current Finality: 32 confirmations are required for transactions, hence the 2 to 12 second finality time.

Kadena

Max tps: There is little testnet information, but with 20 chains on mainnet there have been speeds up to 1000 tps.

Max Theoretical tps: 50000 tps can theoretically be achieved with 1000 chains.

Kaspa

Current tps: The lower part of the range is low likely because relative to some other chains, it's still very early in the adoption cycle and therefore less activity. This could be seen from the Kaspa blockchain explorer.

Max tps: The Kaspa testnet 11 achieves 10 blocks per second to yield 4000 tps.

Max Theoretical tps: Using DAGKnight and 100 blocks per second, it can get to 30000 tps.

Lowest Theoretical Finality: No information could be found, but given the current finality is about 10 seconds with 1 block per second, this will likely be much lower with 10 to 100 blocks per second.

Ethereum

Max tps: There seems to be little information on tps for any of the Ethereum testnets.

Max Theoretical tps: 100000 tps is possible with full danksharding.

Lowest Theoretical Finality: This could be as low as 12 seconds when single slot finality is achieved (in the Ethereum roadmap), rather than the current 32 slots.

Sei

Max tps: 28300 has been quoted as the number for early tests using Sei v2 with Optimistic Parallelization and Sei DB.

Lowest Theoretical Finality: As low as 250 ms has been achieved using Intelligent Block Propagation although there were issues with some nodes maintaining the network and some RPC nodes were lagging behind.

Algorand

Max Theoretical tps: A maximum of 46000 tps could be achieved using a technique known as pipelining.

Current Finality: This is instant finality, hence a value of 0ms.

Pulsechain

Current tps: The lower part of the range is lower than Ethereum mainly because it has less adoption at present. However, Pulsechain is about 17% faster and so the upper range is a little higher.

Max tps: This figure was benchmarked from Pulsechain's testnet v4.

Max Theoretical tps: This is currently unknown although the approach for Pulsechain is that it will implement all the new upgrades and features that Ethereum does. If that happens then this could be the same value as that in Ethereum. However, there is no direct word on this as there is no official roadmap for Pulsechain as such.

Bitcoin

Max tps: There are no figures for maximum tps on any testnets. Perhaps this is not a priority as Layer 2s and sidechains are addressing higher tps.

Max Theoretical tps: For the Bitcoin layer itself there are no known estimates. However, Layer 2s such as Lightning and other solutions like Tectum have an extremely high theoretical tps in the order of millions. In the future, it's possible that changes could be made to the Bitcoin layer itself, but proposals for this are in very early stages and it's not known when this would be scheduled (if ever).

Saito

There is currently no public information on tps or finality for Saito which is still in its early stages of adoption.

Bittensor

Measuring tps for Bittensor to compare against other chains in the table doesn't make too much sense because Bittensor is based more so on events rather than transactions like simple payment transfers. These events consist of machine learning model updates, rewards distribution and consensus activities. This book doesn't cover other AI platforms like Qubic or Singularity NET, so there is nothing to compare it to. However, the Bittensor blockchain explorer currently shows about 2- 10 events per second processed and it's likely that it can process much higher than this when adoption increases.

Current TPS

This shows the number of transactions per second (on mainnet) as a graph taken as a snapshot on a given day from the respective block explorers for those blockchains. Again, it should be noted that the Solana tps is inflated (by about 85%) due to the way it's measured compared to other blockchains (mentioned earlier in the comparison table). Therefore, in the case of Solana the consensus votes have been filtered out for this chart for ease of representation of the bars. Note, that for the comparison table in the previous section they were not filtered out. This provides a general view and will be different on a different day and of course over time these numbers will change with more adoption and scalability improvements.

Note that some of the blockchains covered in this book are not in these charts due to lack of reliable information and some are still very early in adoption.

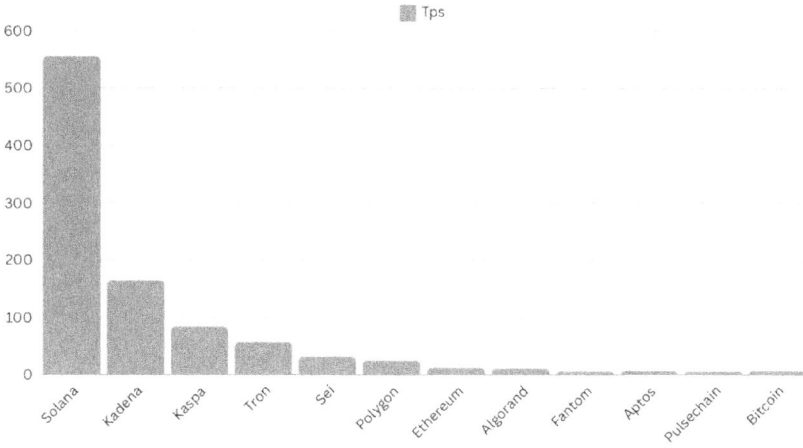

Tps

Daily Transactions

This shows the current number of transactions processed daily by blockchain platform. Note that the number for Solana in this chart is the inflated figure (therefore containing the consensus votes).

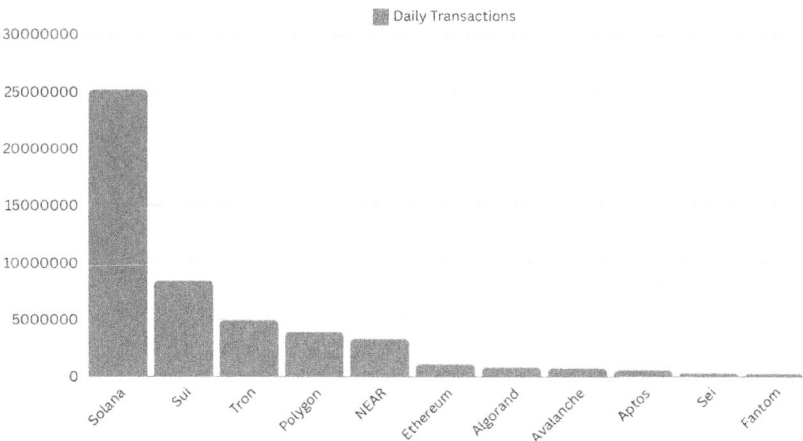

Daily Transactions

Daily Active Users

This shows the number of active users daily for the respective blockchain. Essentially this is the number of unique active wallets each day.

Daily Active Users

References

Most of the numbers for this chapter stemmed from blockchain explorers and official websites for those blockchain platforms. Some of the blockchain explorers and sites are listed here:

Solana stats:

https://solanacompass.com/

Ethereum block explorer:

https://etherscan.io/

Algorand stats:

https://allo.info/

Pulsechain block explorer:

https://scan.pulsechain.com/

Polygon block explorer:

https://polygonscan.com/

Kadena block explorer:

https://explorer.chainweb.com/

Daily Active Users:

https://www.tradingview.com/markets/cryptocurrencies/prices-most-addresses-active/

Special Mentions

There were many blockchain experts who reviewed sections of this book, but I want to say a special thank you to the CEO of Saito, David Lancashire, for sharing his insights and not just reviewing the Saito chapter but other chapters in the book.

I want to thank Randy Daal, the CXO of Kadena, for his enthusiasm on reviewing Kadena and expressing a general interest in the book overall.

I want to show appreciation for Dave Bredson on his ideas and support for the book cover.

About the Author

Ross P. Green is a seasoned professional with a profound journey in the realm of information technology. Graduating from Birmingham University in the UK in 2000, Ross has dedicated over two decades to the ever-evolving landscape of the IT industry.

With a diverse skill set, Ross has navigated various sectors, prominently leaving his mark in Telecommunications and Finance. His extensive experience encompasses roles as a software developer and IT Project Manager, showcasing his versatility and proficiency in addressing the complex challenges of these dynamic fields.

A specialist in backend server software development, Ross has wielded languages such as SQL, C, C++, and Java to craft real-time applications with a focus on multi-threading and cyber security. He has worked on key projects for cyber security in the performance monitoring space, having solid knowledge of symmetric and asymmetric encryption, hashing and key management. His technical acumen and commitment to excellence have been key drivers in his successful career.

Ross's exploration into blockchain began in 2012, marking the inception of his journey into the transformative world of decentralized technologies. His deep understanding of the subject is reflected in his avid reading of various blockchain technology books. This intellectual curiosity has positioned Ross as a thought leader in the blockchain community.

As a figure in the digital space, Ross P. Green has shared his insights on prominent platforms, including YouTube channels such as Sam Stolt's channel. In these appearances, he has provided detailed discussions on Bitcoin development, particularly focusing on RSK (Rootstock). For a closer look at his expertise, you can watch one of his engaging discussions at https://www.youtube.com/watch?v=SRvQgwAZNGQ&t=907s.

Adding to his credentials, Ross holds a Blockchain Certification in IBM Blockchain Essentials, underscoring his commitment to staying at the forefront of technological advancements. His combination of hands-on experience, theoretical knowledge, and effective communication skills makes Ross P. Green a valuable contributor to the ever-expanding dialogue on IT and blockchain technologies.

The Essential Guide to Blockchain Platforms

Embark on a journey into the intricate world of blockchain technologies with The Essential Guide to Blockchain Platforms, a comprehensive guide tailored for beginner and intermediate level blockchain enthusiasts and the inquisitive minds eager to explore diverse blockchain platforms. This insightful book is your go-to resource for understanding the evolution of Layer 1 platforms—from the pioneering ones that emerged alongside Bitcoin to the cutting-edge technologies of today, including Kaspa, Sei, Saito and Bittensor.

Key Features:

Comparative Analysis: Uncover a detailed exploration of various Layer 1 blockchain platforms, providing a comparative perspective that spans the history of blockchain evolution. Delve into the strengths, weaknesses, and unique features that define each platform's contribution to the blockchain landscape.

From Bitcoin to the Future: Trace the developmental journey from the foundational principles embedded in Bitcoin to the latest advancements in blockchain technology. Understand how these platforms have evolved over time, shaping the decentralized landscape we witness today.

Exploring the New Frontier: Journey into the realms of the newest and most innovative platforms, including Solana, Sei and Bittensor. Gain insights into the cutting-edge technologies that are reshaping the future of blockchain and decentralized applications.

Tokenomics Unveiled: While primarily focusing on the technological aspects, the book also offers insightful sections on tokenomics. Understand the economic principles that underpin these blockchain ecosystems and discover how token designs influence the functionality and sustainability of each platform.

This is not just a guide; it's a roadmap for those seeking a deeper understanding of the technological nuances that differentiate blockchain platforms. Whether you're an enthusiast as a beginner or with an intermediate understanding or someone curious about the vast landscape of blockchain technologies, this book equips you with the knowledge to navigate and appreciate the complexities of the ever evolving blockchain frontier. Embark on a journey that transcends traditional boundaries and prepares you for the future of decentralized innovation.

Printed in Great Britain
by Amazon